The Way of the Spiritual Heart

The Journey of Fulfilling Why We Exist

LotusHeart Publishing

Marshall, NC

Ed Rubenstein, Ph.D.

Published by LotusHeart Publishing
255 Sages Way • Marshall, NC 28753-5711

Copyright © 2012 by Ed Rubenstien, Ph.D.

Book layout and design by: Jack Bracewell
Cover backgound image by: Nico Black

ISBN: 978-0-9668700-2-2

LCNN: 2011960321

Book Website
www.WayOfTheSpiritualHeart.com
Email: contact@wayofthespiritualheart.com

Give feedback on the book at:
feedback@wayofthespiritualheart.com

Printed on Demand by
Lightning Source® an Ingram Content Group Company

*Dedicated to
Irmansyah Effendi M.Sc.,
who guided me to realize that
in every moment, True Source,
our Source of Love and Light,
always wants to give the best
of the best to all beings,
you, me and everyone,
on all dimensions.*

Acknowledgements

I would foremost like to thank all Padmacahaya alumni from around the globe who have shared with me the beautiful collective journey of opening our spiritual hearts. Many have contributed constructive feedback and insights which have supported the enfoldment of this book.

My deep heartfelt appreciation to Kathy Cronin, Aile Shebar, Sam Sutker, Jack Bracewell, Al Rubenstein, Carol Lokitz, Arun Rubenstein, Sally Mydlowec, Raven Kelly, James Biddle, Michael Cornelius, Rob Baynes and JaneAnne Narin for helping with the editing, and fine tuning of this book. I am also very grateful to my wonderful wife Paramjit and sons, Arun and Sage, for sharing the joyful journey of letting The Love of True Source open our spiritual hearts.

Table of Contents

Contents

Introduction

Based on your belief system or what you consider spirituality to be, this book may be viewed as radically different. It may challenge how you view yourself, the world, and your understanding of the purpose and meaning of life. It may also challenge how you have been approaching your spiritual journey.

Many of the people who are drawn to read <u>The Way of the Spiritual Heart</u> already know that our spiritual heart is the key to healthy relationships, well-being, true happiness and joy. We may have grown up hearing, "follow your heart" or "listen to your heart". We realize the importance of having a "heart to heart" with someone rather than a "head to head". Our deepest realizations and the meaningful moments in our lives when we are profoundly touched are experienced in our hearts and not our heads. It is not a coincidence that different cultures have phrases such as, "She has a heart of gold", "wholeheartedly", "heartfelt gratitude", and "he has a huge heart".

We are meant to live as a heart. Then, every moment is so special and precious, living life to the fullest with abundant love and joy. To live life from our head is to live a disconnected ego-driven life, missing out on our deepest purpose for being on Earth. Our spiritual heart is the key to spiritual growth and the key for making each moment the precious gift it can be. Many people believe they are already experiencing their spiritual heart; in actuality, however, most of us are in our mind, our head, thinking we are in our hearts. I understand this from personal experience because I did it for many years.

As a Ph.D. Psychologist and spiritual aspirant, I spent over 30 years studying and teaching positive psychology and meditation to people from all walks of life. My pursuit began in the early seventies and led me to study yoga and meditation for nearly three years in Nepal and the Himalayas in Northern India. I also had the opportunity to teach different eastern/western spiritual approaches and meditation modalities in a variety of settings. Throughout that time I believed I was cultivating my spiritual growth. However, I now appreciate that what I was doing – all the disciplines, and all the practices – were actually only cultivating the development of my soul. As I will share with you in this book, I have learned that soul development is not the same as spiritual development.

One purpose of this book is to help explain the difference between soul development and spiritual development. This may challenge the concepts that many of us have regarding the meaning of spiritual growth.

This book is not intended to be a how-to-book. For those who want to go beyond the intellectual understanding, there will be a link provided for participation in Open Heart Workshops. The mind can only grasp a spiritual concept to a certain degree. Our heart is the key to experiencing spiritual realizations from the core of our being.

Spiritual progress can be so very easy and accelerate at a phenomenal rate when our hearts, above all things, realize and experience what it means to trust and accept The Love from The Source of Love and Light. It is my sincere hope that by the time you finish reading this book, you will have a deeper understanding of this most profound truth. You will then understand why only True Source, The Source of Love and Light, can set us free to be who we truly are.

Chapter 1
You Can't Open Your Spiritual Heart

My heart is feeling it is best to communicate with you in a very frank and direct way. I apologize in advance if my directness offends anyone. Our hearts intuitively realize that we are living in a very special time. This means that the way we approach our spiritual journey can now be brought into its truest form. The challenge is that we may have invested a lot of time and energy into a particular spiritual approach or paradigm that once served us but now may limit us, if we continue to pursue our old ways. It is not easy to let go of something we made a strong commitment to. However, when we realize that the practices of the past have served us as a stepping stone to bring us to this special juncture, then we can let go of our old ways with joy. This allows a new spiritual door to open so that we are able to embrace all the profound blessings and gifts from The Source of Love and Light that are being offered to us now.

If you read this book simply to learn new concepts for your mind to consume, you will limit what is being offered. To get the most from these pages, it is best to read with feeling. What does it mean to read with feeling? As your eyes see the words and your mind understands the meaning, let your heart feel and realize the depth of what is being shared.

Are you seeking enlightenment, salvation, yoga, meaning, or understanding the deeper purpose of your life? If so, how will you know it when you find it? Every day I meet people with the same questions that I had; people who are also living in the illusion that they are growing spiritually. Yet, knowingly or unknowingly, they may be trapped in a limited state. This is why I chose to write this book.

Let me ask you another important question: What is the meaning of spiritual growth? How are you measuring your own spiritual development? This is a question I had asked myself since

1972. I had been an aspirant and student of different spiritual traditions for thirty years, and during this time I thought and believed that I had finally found what I wanted. In reality, what I found was an assortment of ways to stroke my ego and build the illusion that I was growing spiritually. I was totally convinced that my measure of spiritual development was genuine. I taught others the spiritual models I was practicing under the belief that these models were a doorway to spiritual fulfillment. I did not realize the limitations of what I was teaching. This is not to say that these different meditation modalities did not have value. It is just that, in regards to spiritual development, they were limited.

Our non-physical heart is a spiritual heart and a true doorway. Yet, even when I thought I was already opening my heart, what I later discovered was that I was merely scratching the surface in a very shallow way.

This book is based on the premise that no human being in history has ever opened his or her heart by earnest effort or by great ability or by special talents. I understand this is a bold statement to make, and from the perspective of the brain, it may not make sense.

Once we realize that opening the heart completely is directly related to the purpose of our existence and that we are not capable of opening our heart by our efforts, techniques and best intentions, then truly, we will never be the same again.

We will embark on a totally new approach to our spiritual journey, with no turning back. The old paradigm of "I can open my heart, and it is up to me to do it," will be challenged. Even when you read that last statement that describes your belief, a big part of you is saying, "Yes...that's right, it is up to me. If it is not up to me, then who will do it for me? If I am going to get somewhere, it is up to me, and I cannot expect or rely on anyone else to do it for me. I am responsible for what I do and create."

Remember, in this life, what we learned is about the positive psychology of the brain that allows us to achieve our goals. We are used to putting the ego in charge, holding the steering wheel of the ship with compass in hand. All we are doing, when we rely on the ego, is enhancing our ability to achieve what we chose to have. The danger of confusing manifesting with spiritual progress is a subject for later discussion, but for now, let me say: *If we have learned how to manifest our highest dreams, but our heart has failed to open, from a spiritual perspective, we have missed the boat.*

Is our heart really open? Consider that just because someone thinks, "My heart is already open and I opened it with my good intentions," does not mean that the spiritual heart has actually opened. *Our spiritual heart is a spiritual heart for one reason only: because the spark of Love and Light from the Source of Love and Light exists in the core of our hearts.* Whatever name for God or Creator you have to represent the Source of Love and Light is irrelevant. This is not about a name. This book is about the greatest gift given to every human being, regardless of culture, religion, race or creed. It is about who we truly are, realizing the purpose of our existence, and remembering the key to true happiness and joy. *Knowingly or unknowingly, when our non-physical heart opens, it is The Love and Light from The Source of Love and Light that opens our heart. It is not our doing, efforts, special talents or ambitions. It is only by feeling and accepting The Love from The Source of Love and Light that our heart opens, allowing us to become who we are in the essence of our being.* This is not about a belief or a conceptual understanding. Authentically opening the spiritual heart is a deep tangible experience.

Throughout the book, I use the term True Source. Since we come from different cultures, religions, and upbringings, the term True Source will be used in this book to represent The Source of Love and Light and The Source of our true selves. Some ask why we don't just use the word "God." God can be a confusing word for many people. History books are filled with examples of countless numbers of people killed in the name of God. In addition, many people rebel against the word God and may even say they are atheists, because they are rebelling against any form of religion or deity, or may have been emotionally traumatized by the version that was imposed on them as a child. Many people have been emotionally damaged by their religious experience and they are still carrying deep unresolved issues related to shame, guilt, fear, anger, unworthiness and confusion. This trauma can block our willingness to love and trust a higher power in this life.

For example, when we feel really hurt by another person, we do not want to greet them with open arms. In the same way, many people have turned away from the concept of God because of their unresolved pain and rebellion against the dogma they were taught. When I have asked atheists if they feel a Source of Love exists, they say they feel it does. They just don't buy the concept of God that was fed to them in their youth. Often, when a person says, "I don't know," it is because their pain has become a defensive wall.

Some of us have issues limiting our spiritual growth because of unresolved issues with our parents. The frustration and other emotions we have with them are then transferred to the concept of a Creator: the Parent of our spark. Our unresolved pain regarding our birth family can also block us from feeling and accepting a relationship with The Source of Love and Light.

It is common for people to have different types of trust issues, and a fear of letting go or losing control. We are attached to our personal agenda, to being in control, and this becomes a key obstacle to our spiritual journey. This will be explored in more detail later on.

The Source of Love and Light is not capable of harm and wants to give us the best of the best in every moment. If we feel ourselves having some resistance to this statement, perhaps it is because we are still holding on to feelings of abandonment, betrayal or rejection left over from long, long ago. These unresolved matters influence the way we relate to True Source. *When our spiritual heart opens more and more, it becomes obvious that True Source has never rejected us. It is we who have rejected True Source's Love by choosing name, fame, power, control, expectations, desires, personal will, self-centeredness, unworthiness, or emotional reactivity over The Love.*

Let us continue our journey in understanding <u>The Way of the Spiritual Heart</u>.

Chapter 2
The Meaning of Spiritual Growth

The beauty of our human family is the diversity of cultural expression in its many forms. Yet beyond all of our differences is an essential unity we share with every being on Earth and beyond.

It has been said that we are not human beings having a spiritual experience; we are spiritual beings having a human experience. A common definition of Spirituality is "an inner path enabling a person to discover the essence of their being." The unity we share is that we all have a spiritual heart and the core of our heart is the spark of Love and Light.

So the big question is, "If we are spiritual beings having a human experience, what is the purpose of our human existence? Why are we really here?"

There are many people who offer answers to these questions, but most often their answers involve a belief system based on concepts of right and wrong, salvation, new age philosophy, and more. Believing in something is not the same as the direct experience of our spiritual hearts. It is also common to think we are in our heart when we may actually be in our mind thinking we are in our heart.

How open our heart will be is dependent on the degree to which our spiritual heart can feel, enjoy and accept The Love and Light of True Source in that moment. The Love that I am describing here is a feeling and not a thought. When we begin to feel our heart, it can seem vulnerable at first, because we may equate opening our heart with emotional pain from previous relationships. This is why it is understandable that some of you may be asking, "Do I really want to open my heart?" "Is it safe to open my heart?" "If I open my heart do I make myself vulnerable and possibly get hurt?"

As our spiritual heart opens we have access to the safety provided by our connection to the Source of Love and Light. When we are afraid of allowing our hearts to open it is because we are confusing the spiritual heart with being emotionally hurt from past relationships.

Some of us are quite confused about who we are and why we exist. We may even come to realize that we are living in a trance, an individualized ersonal soap opera that is unique to us. We may or may not realize there is something more... something beyond our emotional reactivity, the ways our buttons get pushed, our tendency to judge self or others, our likes and dislikes, or the limitations within our minds, as we move from past to present or future identifications and projections. We may or may not know that our sense of 'I' or 'me' is living in a constant state of separation, is a limiting condition or perception, and not the deepest experience of our spiritual beingness.

It is also possible that we are in denial, confusion or puzzlement regarding the purpose of our existence, so we continue to 'look for love in all the wrong places'. Not understanding where we can find True Love, that the source of True Love is within the spiritual heart, we continue to look for love outside of our selves. Our journey can take us through an assortment of adventures as we continue to attempt to find fulfillment in a variety of dead-end roads. The dysfunctional version of this may be found in different forms of addiction ranging from drugs, alcohol, gambling or promiscuity. It can also be the root of codependency or unhealthy boundaries in interpersonal relationships.

Look at the destiny of Romeo and Juliet. The illusion of romantic love led them to seek fulfillment in each other. *It is a trap to expect another to provide the fulfillment that can only be experienced from the direct connection of the core of our heart to The Source of Love and Light.* It really is not fair for anyone to put that grand expectation onto another person. This approach to seeking happiness is guaranteed to backfire. It's just a matter of time.

Another version of 'looking for love in all the wrong places' is about how successful one is in the world. This can include job rank, position, bank accounts, car model, neighborhood, size of house, and other achievements and accomplishments.

Now it all sounds good for someone to have health, wealth, creativity and the ability to achieve or manifest their dreams. The problem is that our focus on achieving all of these accomplishments may have nothing to do with what matters most...and that is the opening of our spiritual heart. We can become so absorbed in fulfilling our needs that our spiritual growth gets squelched. And as we are driven to achieve and manifest more and more, we may find that our arrogance, sense of power and self-importance grows by leaps and bounds. That is why it has been said that power corrupts. Without the humbleness of an open heart and abundant gratitude to The Source of Love and Light for all things, name and fame is a dangerous razor's edge. When our spiritual heart opens more and more, there is nothing for which we are not grateful.

If our accomplishments lead us to realize the limitation of living for the sole purpose of fulfilling our needs, dreams, hopes and expectations, then truly we are ready to wake up from our worldly slumber. If we do not come to this realization, the illusion of achieving and gathering more can drive us to our last breath.

There are dangers in certain aspects of new age philosophy that have become evident in everyday jargon. For example, "I am mastering my ability to create and manifest" or "I know how to use my intention to attract to me what I choose to create." This is often considered by others to be the same as spiritual growth. From the perspective of heart, this is not spiritual growth; it is the growth of our soul, our 'I,' and our ego, and ultimately, what separates us from our Source. True Spiritual growth is the growth of our spirit, our true self, which resides in the core of our heart. Our spirit grows when our heart opens bigger and bigger by feeling, enjoying and accepting The Love and Light of True Source. This is the spiritual process of how we become authentically closer and closer to True Source.

The growth of our spirit, our true self, is directly related to the opening of our heart. This is why allowing True Source's Love and Light to open our hearts is so very important. Even though it may feel normal or logical to our mind to engage in soul enhancement and to cultivate our personal power, following these paths is not why we exist.

Our soul and physical form are gifts provided to us by True Source as vehicles so that our true self, our spirit, can awaken and return Home to its original nature.

Using our intention and our ability to manifest can greatly inflate our soul's sense of power. It is like the moon that begins to think it is the source of the moonlight. When we live for the purpose of soul development, of ego development, we are choosing to turn our back, so to speak, on the True Source of our being. We are denying that the essence of our being comes directly from True Source, and we actually work against fulfilling our true destiny.

The spiritual journey is not about how good we are, how many great deeds we perform or how good we can become. It's not about all the magnificent things we do or how wonderfully we have developed our personal creativity and our ability to manifest our dreams. Neither is it about how bright we can shine. This is all part of a big trap that is easy to fall into since it seems glamorous and can inflate our egos with feelings of righteousness. Real spiritual growth only happens when our hearts open by connecting to True Source's Love, and not by developing our personal soul or ego power. The true expression of spiritual growth is the journey of our spirit, our true self, returning to our Source. It is not the journey of the soul to reach a higher dimension or even the highest heavens. In truth, we cannot have a 'spiritual ego'. Just because we are doing a meditation practice in the name of 'spiritual growth' does not mean that our spirit is growing.

The next five chapters explore five Spiritual Psychology Principles. These principles will help build a foundational understanding about the psychology of our spiritual heart and the spiritual growth process.

Chapter 3

Spiritual Psychology Principle #1

**True Source is The Source of Love and Light,
and The Source of everyone's true self.**

L et us explore a deeper understanding of who we truly are. Calm, peace, joy, true happiness, gratitude and love are the natural feelings radiating from the core of our heart. In our deepest understanding, we come to realize that we are not the originator of these feelings. They don't belong to us. They are radiating through our hearts as a direct result of our connection to True Source.

In the center of our spiritual heart is our true self, also referred to as our spirit. In the deepest core of our true self is our inner heart, the spark of Love and Light from True Source. This is what makes our spiritual hearts so special and this is why people throughout history have known that our heart is the key to our deepest connection to truth. I have heard people say, "I knew it in the core of my heart." I have yet to hear anyone say, "I knew it in the core of my brain." We have a brain, body and soul but these are not who we are. These are gifts from True Source to serve as a facility for our true self to learn and awaken. Our soul and brain are needed for us to incarnate and participate in existence because our true self does not have a form.

Even when we begin to let go of the experience of brain domination and start to feel the spiritual qualities of our heart, we still may not be impressed with the feelings radiating from our heart. Why is it sometimes so difficult to feel with our heart? The reason for this is that our non-physical heart has many layers and these layers contain blockages of energy. These blockages come in many forms and can be considered to be the summary of our ancient journey. When I say 'ancient journey,' some of you may feel what I mean because you can sense that you as a being have existed for much longer than the age of your present physical form. You may even feel your being is much older than Earth. This suggests that the majority of blockages in the inner layers of our non-physical heart have been accumulated over an extended period of time; they did not just originate in the short span of time we have been in our present physical form. If you do not agree with the concept of past lives or reincarnation, please do not let that get in your way with the rest of the book. What we do know for sure, is that our hearts are in bondage, because if there were no blockages in our non-physical heart, True Source's Love and Light would be free to radiate without limit to the hearts of everyone, everywhere.

When I was getting my undergraduate college degree, I became aware that what I thought was reality was only a mirror of my own mind. My belief system, mental concepts, preconceived ideas, judgments, and rationalizations along with unresolved issues and hurts, formed the colored lens through which I viewed reality. It was a wake-up call when I realized that what I considered reality was really a projection of my own mind! I could sense that I was living in a prison constructed by the walls of my ego. Even though my mind was beginning to understand all this, I did not realize that my heart was calling and waiting ever so patiently. As my journey unfolded, I began to sense my heart calling more and more, and I eventually came to realize that my heart and its connection to True Source was the key. However, I was shocked to experience the multi-layered obstructions in my heart. I thought, "If the spark of Love and Light was in the core of my heart, why am I not feeling the gentleness of True Source's Love radiating in all directions?" It was only logical to realize that it was my 'stuff' in the form of impediments that formed dense clouds, shadowing the radiance of the spark of Love and Light within the core of my heart.

Places of un-forgiveness toward others, un-forgiveness toward myself, anger, greed, jealousy, pride, vanity, guilt, shame, feelings of abandonment and rejection, among other emotions were stored as blockages in my non-physical heart.

Our heart develops blockages from the emotional reactivity experienced when our ego and mind are in charge of the show. We do not contaminate the field of our non-physical heart when we are living our life from within our heart.

When we live as if our minds and our thoughts define who we are, we tend to create a number of reasons and excuses for why we have a right to be angry, upset and feel burdened or disturbed. It is so easy to blame circumstances as the reason we are angry, frustrated or upset. The joke is really on us, because on some level, we convinced ourselves that we were benefiting from staying connected to our emotional reactivity. The mind is capable of keeping us convinced to hold onto resentments and un-forgiveness for years and beyond. But, who is suffering from these resentments? That is the irony. We can hold onto our resentments, saying, "They don't deserve my forgiveness." However, we are the ones who are suffering because our emotional reactivity and resentments not only consume huge amounts of energy, but also keep us separated from The Love of True Source.

The real problem is not that we have a mind. Remember, our soul, mind, brain and physical form were given as a gift by True Source, as vehicles to help facilitate our heart to open and for our true self to finally awaken. The problem occurs when we let the ego be the director. When the brain and mind are dominant, the heart remains closed. We are disconnected from our greatest gift and treasure given to us, our hearts.

When we allow The Love to open our hearts by accepting and trusting the Source of Love and Light, the heart invites the brain to become a friend in the service of helping us carry out the orders of our heart. We make positive choices and feel good at the same time. Then, even though we are using our brain, we don't create resentments or fears. We do not contaminate the field of our heart when we are operating from within our heart. We only contaminate the field of our heart when our brain is dominant and our ego is running the show.

By learning to trust, feel, enjoy and accept The Love of True Source, Love radiating from within the heart begins the process of cleansing and dissolving all of our blockages created from living with our ego being in charge. These multi-layered obstructions are our unresolved issues from our past history. Our heart is multi-directional and multi-layered, beyond what our minds can comprehend. True joy arises to the extent that the only thing present in our heart is the radiance of True Source's Love and Light. When we allow all of our unresolved blockages to be dissolved by True Source's Love, then we become who we truly are. No remaining aspect of our being on any level will resist The Love any longer. This is the essence of surrendering.

The process of spiritual surrender is not about what you have to do or give up. It is not something that has to feel like an overwhelming task or something that takes great discipline to achieve. Those approaches to surrender can be a major ongoing battle because one is attempting to use the ego to overcome the ego. Why would the ego be interested in such a deal? In the past, when I attempted to use the mind to tame the mind, I found it to be quite an interesting and futile experience. When we surrender in True Source's Love, surrender is so joyous and profoundly peaceful and gentle. It's like a baby being hugged by a loving mother.

The true path of surrender is simply a process of effortlessly accepting and enjoying the gentleness of The Love on deeper and deeper levels. True Source does not want us to be separate. It is the unresolved blockages we created that are keeping us separate from our true identity as a sweet child of True Source.

The process of surrendering has many levels. The beginning levels of surrender are about letting go of our problems and burdens. They are also about letting go of things we cannot change and accepting the inevitable. For example, this could be releasing the distress we were experiencing when our car broke down or when our pet died. The opposite of surrender would be holding on to our problems, burdens and related distress. If we do not learn to let go of things we cannot change or to let go of things that have happened that we do not like, then our immune system will be challenged. The distress created from our resistance to change can drain our energy reserves. As we progress spiritually, our experience of surrender evolves. This is an evolution from thinking that we have to be the one to do something to surrender, to realizing that when we are open, accept and experience True Source's Love on deeper and deeper levels, everything comes into spiritual alignment. We begin to feel and trust that in every moment, True Source only wants to give us the best of the best. Surrender becomes a joyful reunion and communion with the Source of our being, and all is done for us.

There is a tendency in the new age community to say, "I am God, you are God, we are all God." This is a very risky approach to personal growth, and it will not lead to spiritual growth either. It is worth considering what the ego may be up to during this type of mental dialogue. And it is humbling in an especially sweet way to accept that though our hearts do contain the spark of the Creator, we have a very limited understanding regarding who or what True Source is.

True Source is the One and only Creator of every being. True Source will always be our Parent, and we will always be the children of True Source. The core of our heart is happy to hear these words, though our soul may not be in agreement because of its personal drive or agenda. I share this because it is important to realize that parts of us can be in full agreement with what I am writing. Other parts of us can be in rebellion, or in self-defense for our ego. The parts of us that are in agreement are acknowledging the longing to never be separated from The Love again. The parts that are in rebellion are the drive of the soul, the ego and the 'I' that are still invested in a personal agenda to remain as a separate, independent agent, wandering through the universe believing it is free to do whatever it wants. And it can be a trap thinking that we can help, or be of service to the Source of Love and Light, instead of just dissolving our agenda so we can become a part of The Love.

We were not created to be a 'doer' or to be a 'co-creator'. We were created to enjoy being Loved by True Source and to share The Love. We do not exist so that we can continue expressing and developing our right to be independent and separate from The Love. We exist so that we can learn to let True Source's Love bring us back to where we belong. With that understanding, it is very arrogant for us to think that we know a better way than what True Source, the Source of all of Creation, can do for us. It is time for us to just let True Source's Love do what The Love wants to do, and that is to remove all of our suffering, recent and ancient blockages, and to end the pain of our separation.

Many of us can feel that something very important is about to happen, and is happening. In order to begin the process of coming into alignment with the bigger plan we have to first realize that, **True Source is The Source of Love and Light, and The Source of our true selves.**

Chapter 4

Spiritual Psychology Principle #2

Following the way of our heart brings us to a happy and fulfilled life.

A fish that only knows the boundary of its fish tank cannot realize the splendor of the sea. If we have lived with our heads and brains in charge, we only know the terrain of our ego. What we call happiness, joy or love, is limited to that which our mind comprehends or is capable of experiencing.

Likewise, what we call happiness or love may be a very limited version that is based on our previous experience. Only our heart is capable of experiencing the vast depths of spiritual happiness, gratitude and joy. This is because of our heart's direct connection to The Source of Love and Light. Whatever we may have called a spiritual experience in the past may be just a minor taste of what is awaiting us. When we allow The Love of True Source to open our spiritual heart in all directions, we begin to realize the meaning of True Source's Love in such a way that the soul, ego or 'I' can never ever comprehend. We find ourselves on the freeway Home.

It is not uncommon for us to think we have opened our true heart when in reality we may have just triggered an emotional reflex. When our emotional center has been activated and directed towards another person, this is what we have historically labeled as 'love'. However, this is not the same as opening our spiritual heart by accepting The Love and Light of True Source.

When we feel pain from a relationship that went sour, we often label it as heartache, but it is not our spiritual heart that is hurt. What hurts us are the emotions generated from our ego's attachments, expectations, possessiveness or failed hopes and dreams. Feeling heart-broken is not related to our spiritual heart. It is based on a painful emotional experience and is linked to the energy center in our solar plexus.

On a daily basis we may experience many emotional reactions such as disappointment, frustration, worry, anxiety, and resentment, to name just a few. It is important for us to realize that these emotional reactions are not absolute fact. These reactions are the story line of the personal soap opera we create in any given moment based on how our brain is reacting, or how our emotions are being triggered in that moment. We believe it is real but it is just a story created in the world of our mind.

We make excuses and justifications of why we have a right to these emotional responses. These excuses and justifications are not our friends. They feed upon themselves, fester, and block our journey to become who we truly are. They nourish the ego and they provide the justification to maintain our existence as a separate being. They deprive us of The Love and happiness we long for.

The emotional pains people experience are actually a result of living a brain dominant life and of believing the head is supposed to guide us. But when the brain is the boss, the heart is closed. Know this: the destiny of the brain is always the graveyard. It is just a matter of time. When we let our brain, or mind, be in charge, we believe we exist as an independent agent and fail to realize our intimate connection with life itself.

We create emotional reactions when we are head-centered. Our mind reacts because of thoughts, desires and unsettled memories that activate emotions. Unlike emotions, spiritual feelings are the natural by-product of our heart. The feelings of lightness, expansion, calmness, peacefulness, joy, and love radiate from the core of the heart, because that is where our spark, our true essence resides. The main reason that we do not feel these wonderful feelings is because our head is dominant and the field of our non-physical heart is still contaminated with many layers of blockages.

Lasting happiness cannot be experienced until we allow our heart to be opened. Remember, we cannot open our spiritual heart by our own efforts or techniques. It is only when we let The Love open our heart, then True Source's Love and Light can begin to cleanse everything that is not of The Love. The real 'us', our essence, is in the core of our heart... and as our heart attitude improves from our heart's connection with True Source's Love, the quality of our life and our relationships are enhanced. When we live from deep within our open heart, in addition to enjoying the experience of living in a sacred space where negative emotions do not arise, we continuously enjoy the connection between our heart and True Source. We are brought closer and closer to our Source, our true home, and this is the real spiritual journey.

One of the beauties of opening our spiritual heart is that our heart is not interested in judging others. Instead it flows in rhythm with the waves of life. *For true spiritual growth to occur, the heart needs to become dominant, with the mind working in happy cooperation with the directives of the heart. The mind is meant to serve and support the heart so that we can carry on life being who we really are... a spiritual being in a human body.*

The domination of our mind clouds the radiance of True Source's Love that wants to flow freely and gently from our hearts. Our mind is filled with clouds in many shapes and forms that arise from unresolved issues created when our ego is in charge. These form blockages in our heart. These mental and emotional discomforts arising from the clouds in our mind dirty our non-physical heart. They do not just blow in from the north or south. If they did, we would all be at the mercy of the winds of change; we would be helpless victims without the capacity to choose.

We choose to create the clouds when we live in our heads, and these storm clouds contaminate the field of our heart while also preventing us from feeling the depth of profound joy and love. It is very important for us to realize that we created these clouds when our head was dominant. The biggest trap is thinking the clouds just roll in without our permission. We always have a choice to let our heart feel and accept True Source's Perfect Love instead of identifying with the consciousness of our mind.

Some of you may be thinking that this all sounds nice, but it's not practical, and there is no way you can be in your heart and live in the world. This is the voice of the ego talking and one of the ways the ego likes to justify its existence. The ego wants to convince us that it is really important for the ego to stay in charge, to be the controller of our being. Let us not submit to this argument because it does not serve us. *We can live from our heart in everything we do in our daily lives.* Our heart will not limit us. True Source wants to give us the best of the best in every aspect and dimension of our life. The Love will help us to manage our affairs effortlessly and enjoy life with a better perspective. The benefits are that the quality of all of our relationships becomes enhanced, and our moment-to-moment living will be experienced with deeper significance and true spiritual fulfillment. **Following the way of our heart brings us to a happy and fulfilled life.**

Chapter 5
Spiritual Psychology Principle #3
True Source, the Source of Love and Light,
never wants us separate from The Love.

We have separated ourselves from The Love of True Source by choosing to live a 'head-centered' life. We do not realize the extent of our fear, guilt, shame, unworthiness, or anger. We do not realize the extent of our wounds, traumas, resentments and un-forgiving attitudes toward ourselves and others. True Source's Love wants to do what The Love does, and that is to Love us completely every moment without any exceptions or limitations.

We often feel safe and familiar with our old ways, even though those old ways create mental discomfort, separation and emotional pain. We may have a fear of letting go because we don't know what will happen when we do let go. *That is why it is important to realize that holding onto the need to be in control, or having things be our way, is not a path that leads to ultimate spiritual fulfillment.*

Life can speak to us through other people's pain and we can learn what not to do by observing the painful lessons of others. We can also learn from the imperfections that others may display. What is far more important is not what their imperfections may be, but what our inner tension and reactivity is to our perception of their faults. *Those with whom we find fault are actually our teachers because they show us our patterns of judgment, arrogance and self-righteousness. Those with whom we find fault are also our teachers because our judgmental reactions show us the ways we choose to be separate from The Love. In that moment of judgment, we value our mental position, our ego's perspective, above all else.*

When the head is running the show, judgments can become a habitual pattern that helps the ego to feel good. Our judgments give us a sense of false security, because they create the illusion that others are not as good as we are. The ego, being inherently insecure, also likes to include others in our club, so that everyone who is not like we are may be on some level perceived as less than we are. This is also why it is so convenient for societies to create scapegoats. They get to have someone lower on the ladder in order to produce a hierarchy.

The ego acts as if there is a ladder and it is climbing up it to get somewhere. But it is a ladder to nowhere that continues to engage us, to keep us in our busy-ness, and to guarantee our existence as an isolated being. In the core of the heart, every heart is longing to never again be separated from True Source's Love. Yet when we live our life as if our ego is striving to get "somewhere", we will never really truly arrive. The reason is that there will always be a sense of taking the next step on the ladder and this impulse is what drives our mind. Our ego has created so many ways to continue justifying our experience of living in separation.

The voice that often becomes our greatest teacher is our own pain. Our emotional pain acts as a signal to us that we are not in harmony, and that we are not in our heart. Our ego lives in a state of separation though the extent of this pain can be difficult to recognize because it has become what we consider normal to be. Feeling our pain tells us that we are stuck in our head. It is important to realize that being stuck in our heads is what creates all of the discomfort in our lives. Unfortunately some of us go through life falling into the same holes, living the same patterns, because we fail to realize this. The universe has a way of arranging things so that lessons keep reappearing in different forms. We cannot get away from them.

I grew up in the 1960's in a very dysfunctional neighborhood on the border of the Bronx, New York. Any emotion in the schoolyard other than anger or aggression was considered a sign of weakness. My father had major anger issues which were played out in our family. There is a tendency to adopt patterns that are role-modeled in our home environment. Getting emotionally triggered and responding by getting 'pissed-off' seemed quite normal in mine. "If only they stopped doing that, I wouldn't get so angry," was my justification. It was never about me. It was always about them. People or circumstances were the cause of my anger. I felt I was a victim. This pattern followed me and reappeared in different permutations and with different people until I realized I was the one who created the experience of anger. It was my reactivity that resulted in anger; it was not the fault of the circumstances.

Wherever we go, life will be there waiting for us with similar problems and similar lessons until we have learned to allow The Love to open our heart and choose True Source's Love in all instances. This is the primary lesson for us to learn. Developing insight and realizations from our heart helps us recognize the gifts from the lessons life offers.

In the past I engaged in different modalities and psychotherapeutic approaches to address core personality patterns. I found benefit in these approaches but they were only able to bring me so far. Although I came to understand my patterns and reduce their influence, just knowing about them or being able to observe them, did not free me from them. Only after I learned to trust and accept The Love on a deep level, I experienced a freedom from core personality and ego patterns.

So let's review what we have been discussing. What is a blockage? *A blockage in the field of our heart is anything that keeps True Source's Love from radiating sweetly, gently and completely to every being, in every direction, on every dimension in the whole existence. Blockages are only present because they exist in separation from The Love. True Source never wants us to be separate from The Love and wants to dissolve all of the obstacles we have accumulated.*

How does The Love from True Source work? The nature of The Love is that it never pushes and is always the most gentle. Therefore, Love will not force us. We have to be a willing participant and we do that by learning not to 'try' or 'do,' but simply to 'feel' and 'let' our heart accept the gift of Love that awaits us in every moment; allowing The Love to clean us and to do what it Will. This is so different compared to attempting to use our mind to create a change in the ego. When the ego is running the show, there is often a never-ending cycle of pressure to change, trying to change, and a sense of failure that we have not properly succeeded.

No human can ever touch us, hug us or embrace us the way the sweet gentleness of True Source's Love can. When our heart begins to accept The Love from the direct connection of True Source, The Love will continue to dissolve all blockages and everything that is not of The Love. We naturally continue to grow in the realization that True Source's Love never wants us separate from The Love. Our heart knows the huge mistakes we have made in the past, when we chose our ego's position over the gift of True Source's Love and Light. Once we begin to experience the beauty and joy that awaits when allowing True Source's Love to open our heart, our heart will never want to be separate from True Source's Love again. **True Source, the Source of Love and Light, never wants us separate from The Love.**

Chapter 6
Spiritual Psychology Principle #4
Our deepest purpose on Earth is to share The Love of True Source, by allowing our hearts to radiate The Love to all hearts in existence.

We are being called to be instruments of True Source's Love. This is exactly the way True Source designed us. In being an instrument, we can experience joy and freedom on a level beyond anything the mind is able to conceive.

What does being an instrument mean? *We become an instrument of True Source's Love by enjoying, feeling and accepting The Love of True Source, not by being the 'doer' in charge of the process.* For example, typically when people pray or meditate, they experience themselves as being the one meditating, which means they are the 'doer' of the meditation. Enjoying, feeling and accepting The Love of True Source is not something we do; it is an "experience" that just happens on us. The Love of True Source is always given freely to every being. The question is: "What is it in us that does not allow us to receive the full blessing of this gift?" Why are we placing limits on how much of The Love we let ourselves experience? This will be addressed in later chapters.

In all of our human relationships it is important to have healthy interpersonal boundaries. Without them we get our buttons pushed in a variety of ways. *Our heart relationship with True Source is the only relationship that is truly safe and where it is totally advisable to let go of all boundaries.* When we begin to experience the heart, we realize that we create boundaries or have edges in place. The ways we have created these edges are related to our past pain from interpersonal relationships and the way we have learned to stay separate from The Love. Dissolving the boundaries of our non-physical multidirectional heart happens when we let go of our defensive armor. This armor is the way we protect our definition of who we think we are. *We create armor because we fear what will happen if we allow ourselves to be loved completely.*

An aspect of our ego thinks, "If we let go completely, we will fail to exist. So, it really is not a good idea to totally trust The Love of True Source." We hold onto the boundaries around our heart because we have a fear of losing control. From the perspective of the ego, we must strive to maintain control; from the perspective of The Love, we know control is an illusion that keeps us separate from the Love itself.

Once the illusion is unveiled, we see that the more the ego wants or needs to be in control, the more the ego actually spins out of control. This is because it is acting from a place of reactivity and a need to defend its boundaries. And even though the ego may appear "healthy" and have well-developed means to protect itself, the more it defends its boundaries, the more out of control it really is. The ego typically prevents us from realizing the extent to which we live in isolation, lonely, disconnected, and marooned from The Love True Source wants for us.

We tend to hold onto the idea of control, because we have convinced ourselves that this is how we remain free to be 'who we are'. But what we are protecting by our sense of control is not who we really are, but a poor imitation of who we really are. It is like spending our life guarding and defending what we think is a treasure, and then finding out it is not really a treasure but something bogus, holding us back from experiencing the greatest treasure of all. Our greatest treasure is the spark of Love and Light within our hearts.

We have to realize that the limiting boundaries on our multi-directional non-physical spiritual heart are the result of allowing our ego to keep us from our true treasure. In addition, when our egos are in charge, we continuously create obstructions that are stored in the inner layers of our heart, and these are the 'clouds' blocking the sunlight of True Source's Love from freely radiating in and from our hearts.

When we begin to rely on The Love of True Source, our spiritual hearts begin to open. We realize The Love of True Source is not something to be stored or collected for a rainy day. Attempting to store it actually limits the flow because The Love of True Source is designed to be shared. Healthy parents want their children to let go of sibling rivalry, and emphasize sharing love with one another and this is the same for us as children of True Source, that our Parent wants us to love each other.

Our bottom line identity is that we are sparks of True Source and as the children of True Source, we are meant to share The Love of True Source to the heart of every being on every dimension, with no exceptions. To allow this spiritual evolutionary process to unfold is the fulfillment of our true nature. When we block this process and stay attached to our own agenda and our ego's ways, we fail to realize that every heart, every being, in the whole existence is our sibling and part of our family. Even if others are having temper tantrums or living in a state of rebellion, they are still a part of our family. If they are choosing poorly and rejecting Love, True Source loves them as completely as True Source loves a saint, just as True Source has always loved us unconditionally and completely... regardless of our attitudes and behaviors.

If we are to be an instrument for True Source's Love flowing through our heart, who are we to say who True Source should love and who True Source should deny? Any time we block or refuse to share the gentleness of True Source's Love, we suffer from creating an impediment to The Love.

In order to allow True Source's Love and Light to radiate to the heart of all beings, our heart has to open in all directions. This means opening completely left to right, front to back and up and down. This is the only way we can become instruments for the heart of all beings, just as True Source wants us to be. And the best news is that all we need to do is to not do, but to allow it to happen. When our heart is in proper connection with The Love, we are able to relax completely and let go of trying or doing. When feeling and enjoying The Love, then The Love of True Source takes care of everything for our whole heart and whole being.

Many people feel a burning question that they yearn to have answered. The question is, "True Source, what is my primary assignment on Earth?" This question is easy to answer because *we all have the same primary assignment. We are here to be instruments of True Source's Love and Light. Whatever we do in the world, whatever projects we take on, are secondary to our true purpose on Earth.*

Some may ask, "How can I be an instrument of True Source's Love and Light when I have a full-time job and so many other duties and responsibilities in the world?" When we learn to rely on True Source's Love above all things, our hearts are grateful for every moment we choose True Source's Love over our ego's agenda. Being an instrument is not meant to be reserved for those quiet times when we get a chance to close our eyes. When our heart realizes what it means to rely on True Source's Love, we can learn to remain as instruments during our waking hours in all that we do. This is something that can be so easy, natural and effortless even while engaging in all physical and mental activities because The Love never wants us separate from The Love. It is 'us' that creates the separation. The Love is always waiting to bring us back to where we belong when we stop resisting by being the one 'in charge'.

My heart is very grateful as I remember how I used to experience my daily life in contrast to how I experience it now. In the past, it seemed as if I was always moving forward to reach something that was ahead of me. My sense of arrival was always short-lived, and then I was reaching again to what still lay ahead of me. And things seemed 'ahead' because I was living from my head and this was driving my life.

Part of me was always trapped in the future and not available to be completely present in the now. My experience of reality is completely different since I have allowed The Love of True Source to bring me into the experience of my heart. I still have goals along with to-do lists, and I lead a productive life. However, the mental drive of moving towards the fulfillment of my goals is transformed into the experience of moment-to-moment heartfelt gratitude. Driving, working, filling out paper work, interacting with others, learning new things and doing the dishes can be so joyful when they are experienced from our heart instead of our heads. Life becomes a beautiful flow. This is the process of becoming an instrument while in motion and functioning in our everyday lives, even while engaging in things that we may have previously thought of as mundane.

The more we feel, enjoy and accept True Source's Love, the sweeter and gentler True Source's Love is shared for the benefit of all beings. What a great arrangement True Source has given us! The more we enjoy True Source's Love, everyone benefits. As we allow The Love to radiate through us, we begin to let go of all our fears and limitations in sharing love with others. As we become sweeter instruments, we begin to let The Love impartially touch every being and every event in existence. There is no way any of us could come up with a better deal than this. As The Love is radiating through our heart to the hearts of others, their hearts begin to awaken. Without words, our hearts naturally extend the invitation we feel and enjoy from True Source to others, inviting their hearts to open. When we are instruments, The Love also begins to dissolve all of our blockages so that we do not have to suffer from separation from The Love.

When I first began allowing The Love to open my heart, I was only comfortable feeling a limited amount of joy. I guarded how much I was willing to feel and experience True Source's Love because of patterns of unworthiness that I did not even know existed. As an instructor of Open Heart Workshops, I have heard from many participants that they also feel very limited in how much Love and joy they are willing to feel and accept. A probable reason for this limiting tendency is that from our past lives, we inherited negative patterns that cause us to feel unworthy of being loved. There may also be old feelings of anger, doubt or being abandoned or rejected by True Source -as if to say, "God, why did you let me down?"

When we get to experience the gift of being an instrument of True Source's Love, we realize that the more we enjoy and accept The Love, the more all of our siblings everywhere will benefit. The radiance of The Love has a positive effect on our immediate environment and beyond. Negative energies are neutralized or transformed in ways we may not even be conscious of. Being an instrument allows us to bypass our sabotaging blockages that keep us feeling unworthy of True Source's complete Love. By enjoying The Love, grateful for the opportunity to be an instrument of The Love, feeling grateful that True Source's Love is being shared with all beings, our own unworthiness begins to dissolve. This is such a wonderful process. Being an instrument sets our own heart free. Sharing The Love with others helps us to develop a deeper understanding and appreciation for The Love. This is also the time in which we are accepting True Source's Love better and better. **Our deepest purpose on Earth is to share The Love of True Source, by allowing our hearts to radiate The Love to all hearts in existence.**

Chapter 7

Spiritual Psychology Principle #5

When we learn to live in our heart and trust and enjoy The Love of True Source, The Love will bring our true self Home to be a part of The Love.

From the moment we felt our separation, True Source has wanted us to come Home in the here and now, to once again become a part of The Love. This joyful journey of our spirit, our true self, returning to our Source, is what spiritual growth is all about, and the reason for our entire journey. In such a gentle and beautiful way, True Source wants to dissolve the hindrances accumulated over the course of our long journey, which were created when our ego was in charge.

We contaminated the field of our hearts, not when we were grounded in our hearts, but for the eons when our ego ran the show. All of our blockages, which are sometimes referred to as karma, are not something to fear or be ashamed of. When we realize that the perfect and unfaltering Love from True Source wants to help us in every moment, it is something to celebrate and rejoice with never ending gratitude. After so very long, finally, we can let True Source's Love clean us up and bring us Home to who we truly are.

All True Source wants to do is to Love you, me and everyone completely in every moment... always, and far beyond what our brain or ego can ever imagine. Our boundary is our resistance to letting True Source Love us the way The Love is intended to do. When our heart begins to feel, enjoy, trust and accept True Source's Love, the non-physical boundary of our spiritual heart begins to open and expand. As we let The Love give us the best, then The Love begins to set our heart free. This is the direction of the true freedom that the core of every heart knowingly or unknowingly seeks. *Everything not of True Source's Love forms the armor that keeps us within a rigid boundary, along with the layers of blockages that maintain the separation.*

We do not realize all the ways we are limiting True Source's Love. An example of how we limit is when we take credit for our spiritual progress. All credit is due to The Love of True Source. When we take credit for our good deeds and intentions, it simply strengthens the will of the soul, our ego identity and our arrogance. We can easily convince ourselves that we are doing good things, or 'heading' in the right direction. However, from the perspective of true spiritual growth, we may be fooling ourselves. I feel it is important for us to realize that we have created a box of limitations made by our habits, ways, thinking patterns and ego concepts. Inside this box we could remain trapped by our own creation without recognizing that we have created such a confined space. It can seem so normal because this is the place we function from in our everyday lives.

The path of True Source's Love and Light is the direct path Home to who we truly are. True Source's Love and Light is the Highway. *Our path Home is tricky because there are many exits along the journey that can take us off the main Highway of True Source's Love.* These exits can have glamorous attractions that are actually big pot holes contributing to the illusion that Home could be something other than True Source's Complete Love. For example, I have already shared how it is possible to confuse our ability to create and manifest as being the same as spiritual growth. This is an exit off the Highway of True Source's Love that can give us the feeling that we are co-creating with God.

In actuality, all that is taking place is the fulfillment of one's desires, hopes, expectations and dreams. This grows the power of the soul to manifest what it chooses to create. It can be intoxicating when one gets to bathe in the awe of what seems to be created by his or her intentions. We may pay lip service to the concept of the Will of True Source, but unless we are humbly being led by The Love, we may actually be creating further separation from our Source. In the name of co-creating with God, the ego takes the opportunity to play out its agenda and demonstrate its right to exist as an independent agent, basking in the glory of its creations.

We were not created to demonstrate what we can do or achieve. Neither are we here to perfect our way of using our will, our intention, to circulate energy or to achieve great feats of energetic mastery. Many of us have come to realize that we have tried all of that and more during the course of our long ancient journey, and it has not gotten us one millimeter closer to our Creator. In fact, following our hopes, wills and desires have gotten us farther and farther isolated from True Source. *We are on this dimension to learn to feel, enjoy, trust and let The Love heal everything we created that is not of The*

Love, so that True Source's Love and Light can bring us and all beings Home to our true nature.

It is so easy for us to get consumed by searching for spiritual fulfillment in an assortment of places. For example, many may think that being mindful or fully present in the 'here and now' is the ultimate spiritual goal. Others of us believe that connecting and feeling at-one with nature is what the spiritual journey is all about. Some of us may think getting in touch with our guardian angel, developing intuition, opening our third eye, experiencing the space between our thoughts and breaths, communicating with non-physical teachers or ascending to a higher dimension are the means by which we spiritually progress. From my experience and from my heart's best understanding, these are all examples of exits on the Highway of Love that can take us off-track and lead us down dead-end roads. These excursions can be stimulating, entertaining, and fascinating because the vastness of non-physical dimensions can be very attractive. They can also be addictive. This especially applies to approaches that cultivate energy. If we feel we are becoming a more powerful being, it is easy to convince ourselves that we are moving in the right direction. We can be very sincere, want to help others and have the desire to grow spiritually. Still, we must realize the difference between the trap of soul enhancement and the true goal of spiritual growth.

The excursions that I previously mentioned are examples of soul development. How enticing it can be to engage in spiritual shopping. This means going from one group, technique or workshop to the next, trying out many different approaches. When we do this we are seeking and satisfying some curiosity, but we may not really know what it is we are looking for. Some are searching for truth while others are looking for new adventures or greener pastures. At times, we may stay with one path even though we admit we have hit a plateau and feel stagnated. Our predicament may be that we are following a limited approach in regard to spiritual development. We are relying on a technique or a process in which we are the 'doer' in charge and may lack the realization that our heart is the key to our connection with True Source. This sacred connection is not based on how hard we try, or how good we can get at a technique or practice but on our willingness to trust, feel and accept The Love of True Source with abundant gratitude.

As previously explained, spiritual growth is directly related to the spark of Love and Light in the core of our hearts and not about the development of the ego and soul. It is directly linked to allowing

The Love to open our hearts resulting in the growth of our spirit, our true self. Only True Source's direct Love and Light can do this. All of our own efforts, no matter how good our motives may seem, limit the growth of our spirit because we are focusing on our ways, rather than the way of The Love. When we exit the highway of True Source's Love, whether we know it or not, we are looking for The Love in all the wrong places.

Even when doing wonderful projects that help others, our actions can be driven by the drive of the ego. Some of us may become consumed with thinking and feeling, "There is so much I have to do to help and serve others." It is wonderful to be of service to others, although it is important to realize two things. First is that our service needs to flow from our hearts and not from our egos. And second, when we have learned to trust The Love and to be instruments of The Love, True Source's Love can radiate and be of service to the planet and beyond, even when we are going about our daily tasks of living. This means while washing the dishes, driving our car, waiting in line or paying our bills, we can remain in alignment with True Source's Love, as The Love radiates to all beings.

We have a tendency to think, "I know what is best." You may be able to feel a part of you saying, "Yes, of course...if 'I' cannot know what is best for me than who does?" The problem is that the part of us that thinks we know best is the 'doer' that does things our way. This same attitude is what many of us bring into the approach of our spiritual journey. "I am choosing how to pray and meditate." "I am getting better at meditating and getting more committed and disciplined." "I will get to my spiritual goal by my determination." *The essence of this book is that it is time for us to let go of this attitude and approach, which limits true spiritual growth. Our ways, habits and ego patterns are so ingrained with this style that we have come to believe that this attitude of being in charge is a necessary fact and the way it has to be in order to grow spiritually. Therefore, we just keep doing it the way we understand, and often without question.*

Many people I have met share a common view that the Source of existence is just "energy" and therefore "neutral". As a result of this concept, they think that we must take charge, and that as we think and intend, the Source adds energy to our thoughts. It is as if God is impartial to our thoughts, and amplifies our thoughts whether they are positive or negative. The emphasis of life becomes on creating the destiny of our choice. There was a time when I used to also believe a similar version of this understanding. *A profound shift in my being took place when my heart realized that the balance of existence, and the flow of the seasons, is not just held together by the balance of forces. The core of my heart realized that The Love of True Source is not just an intelligent form of energy, and True Source has a Will and Purpose. True Source is waiting for our whole heart and whole being to come into complete alignment with The Love. Our soul's ability to create, manifest, and build its ranking in existence, is not why we exist.*

As the heart opens, and we begin to realize and experience the wondrous gifts of The Love that are offered continuously to us, we reach the profound and liberating point of asking, "Who are we to think that anything we do on any level is better than what The Love of True Source can do for us?" Each of the ways in which we have been in charge of the process is an exit off the Highway of True Source's Love. When our heart truly realizes what it means, after so very long, to be on the Highway of The Love, it will begin to feel painful when we exit the path. And when we do get pulled into our old ways and habits of thinking we know best, we will not want to stay gone for very long because we realize we would be turning our back on True Source's Love.

It is time for us to learn to totally trust The Love. If we cannot trust The Love of True Source, what can we trust? Everything else we have, the ego and the brain, is temporary and just a passing show. Anything of this Earth and any relationship will soon be gone just as we will disappear from Earth. History has shown us this fact. The Love of True Source is eternal and what our heart seeks, and The Love of True Source is always waiting to embrace us, just as if we are babies being hugged by the most loving Mother.

The spiritual journey is simply about trusting The Love and trusting the direct connection that the core of our heart has with True Source, the Source of Love and Light and the Source of our true selves. *When we allow The Love to help us trust, enjoy and accept True Source's Love with complete gratitude, then The Love will dissolve everything that is not of The Love. We will have no issues with anyone, anywhere on any dimension, and our heart will be free to let True Source's Love and Light radiate to the heart of every being in the whole existence without exception. This is the essence of what it truly means to experience forgiveness at the deepest level.*

This means that the sweetness and gentleness of True Source's Love that radiates to our friends and family is no different than the gentleness of Love that radiates to every being, including those beings on lower dimensions. What I have just shared may sound like an overwhelming task to achieve. But remember, we are not the 'doers.' *And we are unable to do this because we do not have a clue as to where 'every being' is. As we learn to rely on The Love, The Love can radiate through us naturally, gently and effortlessly. As we feel, enjoy, trust and accept The Love of True Source with abundant gratitude, we realize on deeper and deeper levels that True Source has never wanted us separate from The Love.* Rather than resist the spiritual process, we are then able to rely on and let The Love do what The Love has always wanted to do. That is, to clean us up and bring us Home to our true nature of never being separated from The Love again. *This is the meaning of spiritual growth; the journey of our spirit returning to our Source. Experiencing this fulfills the journey of why we exist.* **When we learn to live in our heart and trust and enjoy The Love of True Source, The Love will bring our true self Home to be a part of The Love**

Now that we have explored the five Spiritual Psychology Principles, let us continue our journey to better understand the psychology of our spiritual heart.

Chapter 8
Our Great Gift of Choice

It is beyond our comprehension to grasp how True Source created all of existence. The grand intelligence behind everything leaves us in awe. A little bird can fly south across oceans and mountain ranges and return to the same nest the following year. Our fingernails grow back after we cut them. Our being knows how to breathe even while we sleep. The Earth and other planets in our solar system know their paths around the sun and our sun knows how to follow its larger orbit through our galaxy. Our galaxy is one of billions all pulsing in accordance with something vast and unseen.

Yet, here we sit on this little planet caught up in our different personal agendas while our ego is industrious with its busyness. While engaged in the many preoccupations of our ego, we miss out on what is the deepest and most profound inner calling of our being.

The most profound of all the profound wonders in the whole of existence is that, within the core of our spiritual heart, there is a spark of Love and Light from the Source. This spark is a gift of love from the Source of Love and Light. Our spark is the core of our true self, and directly experiencing this spark is what truly matters above all things.

As long as it lives, that little bird that flies across the ocean will always be just a bird. Even if it wants to change its bird mind, it will remain within the constraints of the instincts birds are designed to have.

What is it that gives us our spiritual uniqueness among all creatures on Earth? It is our capacity to choose and to prioritize. *Our ability to choose and prioritize is executed by our free will and this is what determines and guides our destiny. We can use our free will to remain separate from The Love or we can use it to choose to embrace and accept True Source's Love. The greatest choice we can make is when we use our free will to choose True Source's Love above all things. Making this choice is the most important thing we have to do in this life!*

This is not about just choosing True Source when we meditate or pray. It is about choosing True Source's Love in every moment, and, making the choice in a way that is not a struggle or difficult to make. When we are embracing and accepting The Love, The Love instantly helps and guides us into a direct connection with True Source's Love. In this direct connection, there is a feeling of complete and everlasting joy. Feeling this complete joy makes the whole process of embracing and trusting The Love easy and effortless. As we get past our fears of letting go deeper into The Love, we experience True Source as the Most Loving One above all, who always gives us the very best.

This can only happen when our whole heart and whole being have prioritized the importance of choosing The Love above our wanting to execute our free will. It is free will, in fact, that causes us to remain a being living in separation. When we prioritize True Source's Love above all things, our heart becomes so strong in the gentle sweetness of Love that it becomes painful to leave.

Even when we attempt to choose something that is out of alignment with The Love, The Love is always present, gently inviting us to reconnect with the true nature of our spiritual hearts.

When we use our free will to stay in separation, we remain as an independent agent addicted to our own agendas, while we wander through existence chasing our hopes, wants and desires. And we can be in separation, with our own agendas, while thinking, while believing, that we are growing spiritually.

When we are using our free will, our past experience is like a hamster that runs around a ferris wheel, believing the wheel will lead it out of its cage. No matter how hard and fast it runs, the mouse still remains on the wheel and in its cage. Personal agendas are quite tricky because they can have us convinced that we are following them for a righteous or noble reason, or that we are doing what we are supposed to be doing. We fail to see that we are attached to a certain outcome and have chosen our agenda over choosing The Love.

If we do not find the sweetness of contentment in our heart, then the outside world will always seem like it is filled with problem after problem. When our heart is fulfilled, our contentment does not come from the world. Only the connection of our heart to True Source will bring the deepest level of happiness, what we have been yearning for... a yearning to no longer be separate from The Love itself. It is only then that we begin to be 'in the world but not of it'.

Free will gives us the ability to choose, and our choices can be detrimental to our spiritual well-being. Seeking sex, money, control, and power in different shapes or forms are the biggest traps that humans fall into, throughout history. It should be obvious that relying on these choices for contentment sends us on a wild goose chase that will inevitably lead down a dead end road. A false and fleeting sense of success is thus based on what we have, or what we do, and not who we are when we are surrendered to The Love.

We exist for spiritual success, not just worldly success. True success is based upon a deep connection between our heart and True Source, The Source of Love and Light, and the Source of our spirit, our true self. Our achieving excellence and a level of spiritual success depends upon the quality of our heart connection. It is not about 'us' or our sense of accomplishments.

Remember what was said earlier: when we choose to trust and accept Love, we let The Love of True Source open our hearts. We don't open our hearts. Choosing The Love does.

As our hearts open bigger, simultaneously our spirit, our true self enjoys embracing The Love. Our true self wakes up and moves closer and closer to True Source. However, due to our conditioning, we are at risk of taking life for granted and sleeping through our time on Earth. Instead of using the gift of choice and our free will to choose True Source's Love, we may remain stuck in our heads. Our ego then brings us on a journey to fulfill its needs, wants, desires, expectations, hopes, and dreams.

There is a common misconception of what it means to be free. But, as True Source's Love opens our spiritual heart bigger and bigger, we begin to realize that what we thought was our right to freedom is actually the bondage and imprisonment of our ego. With the ego running the show, our emotional reactivity and poor choices contaminate the field of our heart. This contamination, this accumulation of karmic blockages from our past bondage to our ego, keeps us in separation from True Source's complete Love.

By feeling, trusting, enjoying and accepting True Source's Love with gratitude, we are open to letting The Love clean up the mess we created when our ego was the chief in charge. True freedom is the freedom of our spark to never again be separated from True Source's Love. The core of our hearts realize what this means in a way that our ego or mental concepts could never conceive.

Chapter 9
The Automatic Pilot Function of the Ego

It is easy for us to get set in our ways, habits and concepts because that is what feels normal and makes up the fabric of what we consider to be reality. Spiritual progress takes place when our spiritual heart opens more and more. As we continue to enjoy and accept True Source's Love, the Love takes us into the deeper inner layers of our non-physical heart.

As we begin allowing The Love to open our spiritual hearts we may encounter deep resistance. We have to be willing to let go of our old ways, concepts and habits. When our head is in charge, our ego has its own unique way of recreating patterns such as worry, dissatisfaction, arrogance, fear, insecurity, greed, and so on. In addition, our ego has a tendency to hold on to resentments. We can train the ego to think more positively but we cannot train the ego to let go of its identity as a separate entity. To do so would be like asking water to no longer be wet.

I have had clients ask me if I would help hypnotize them or put them into a trance. I smile and say in the gentlest tone possible, that actually I do not have to do this because they are already in trance; the trance of their fears, worries, insecurities, judgments, greed and all the other mental preoccupations and emotional reactions they experience in their moment to moment lives. If we honestly examine the consciousness patterns of our ego on a typical day, we will come to understand that much of our mental and emotional makeup runs on automatic pilot.

We may think we are in charge, but are we really? The reason I say this is because the automatic-pilot feature of our ego brings our attention to thoughts and emotions that we are not choosing to experience. One moment we can be frustrated over something that happened a week ago and the next moment we fear a root canal appointment coming up at the end of the month. The next moment we can be angry because we think the car mechanic charged us too much money to fix our brakes and a moment after that we are feeling proud of our son who made the honor role at school. Two minutes later we doubt ourselves and the next moment we are on cloud nine thinking about the concert we are going to see that evening. Within a ten minute period our minds can take us on a roller coaster ride of mental trips and emotional swings. We do this in many different ways. This goes on automatically, continuously, throughout the day, from the time we wake up until the time we go to sleep. Did we give ourself permission to go to all these places? If we are honest about ourselves, the answer is no.

For the most part, our mental preoccupations and emotional adventures just happen without our permission. It is as if our thoughts are thinking us.

When we get triggered, we do not say, "Now I am choosing to spend the next five minutes in worry, judgment or anger." But if an emotion starts to feel out of control, we need to have a way to talk with ourselves to bring things back into check. This can keep us from doing things that are too rash or that we would regret.

Usually we have a self-monitoring system to make sure our thoughts and emotions do not get too out of hand. Even though we can be raging on the inside, most of us have enough control to not externally express it. We have learned to execute impulse control so that our drive or urges do not take over. However, at times we cannot hold on anymore, and maybe we explode outwardly even when we want to control ourselves. Some of us keep our impulses in control because our police and our laws create 'do's and don'ts' to keep us in check. *Our heart naturally has a conscience that knows proper actions and responses that are in harmony with the present moment.*

We act as if our ego is a solid fixed entity, but it is really quite fragmented. What is the 'real' ego, if the ego can express itself so differently from one moment to the next and often does so without our conscious awareness? *We put a make-believe circle around the multiple fragments and expressions of the ego and say, "This is who I am." Then we move and act in the world as if we know who we are. We defend our turf, our ways, habits, desires and concepts. We fail to realize that our ways, habits and unresolved issues define and defend our ego and fuel its unique automatic pilot function.*

The ego plays out different dramas in life based on the assortment of ways we get triggered. It then calls this dramatic episode a reality, or a truth. The ego fails to realize that what it sees and how it reacts is directly related to the stories we tell ourselves, stories made up from the scripts we have written from our minds: our habits, concepts, hurts and resentments, successes or failures. *We think we're seeing and experiencing the world as it is. But in reality we're seeing the world only as it is reflected through that loop, the ferris wheel of habit and expectation, thinking we are moving when we are running in place. We see the world through the colored lenses worn by our minds.*

When we continue to live as if our ego is who we are, than we will not be able to let True Source's Love and Light open our spiritual hearts. *We have to be willing to let go of who we are not, in order to let The Love help us become who we truly are.* This is the spiritual challenge that awaits us. As we open more and more to the process, the fear of change, the feeling of challenge, are transformed into great joy, and we feel the quality of our heart's awakening.

As we feel our hearts open, letting go of our old habits and ways, those old stories and dramas, we become more natural, and letting go becomes the most enjoyable thing to do. In the Fall, the oak tree releases all of its leaves to the ground without resistance. Those leaves then become nutrients in the Earth to help the tree grow. Likewise, when we let The Love help us remove what is not of The Love, then our spiritual hearts open and our true selves can grow in True Source's Love and Light.

The releasing of our ego patterns not only helps our hearts to grow in many ways, but helps others as well. For example, experiencing the different types of pain our ego creates, helps us to better understand the pain that others are going through. Similarly, as *more of us let The Love help us to let go of our ego patterns, while choosing True Source's Love as our priority, then it becomes easier for other beings to do the same.* The reason this happens is because everyone is spiritually connected. We are spiritually connected because we are all created from the One and only Source above all.

As more and more of us allow True Source's Love and Light to open our spiritual hearts, a collective spiritual flow is created. This collective spiritual flow makes it easier and easier for all hearts to love and trust True Source as our natural, true way of being. Rather than our ego running the show on automatic pilot, our hearts will naturally and effortlessly express gratitude. True gratitude, as a natural expression of loving True Source, helps us to embrace and accept True Source's Love even more.

Chapter 10
The Gift of Recognition

In order to utilize the great gift of choice, we have to understand what it means to be in tune and what it means to be out of tune. We have to recognize that at any moment there are two basic choices. Choice one is that we choose to remain in our minds, preoccupied and busy with our personal agendas. The ego is in charge. Choice two is we choose the path of True Source's Love, which brings us deeper into our hearts, so that we can become an instrument aligned with True Source's Love.

Even when we learn to effortlessly experience the gentleness and joy of The Love in our hearts, it does not necessarily mean we can transfer this experience to our everyday moments of daily living. When we hear a piece of music we enjoy, we can tell if it is being played out of tune. The reason we can do this is because we have a reference point. We know what it sounds like when the song is played in tune. Likewise, we have to recognize very clearly when we are in tune and when we are out of tune with The Love. When we first recognize that our mind is running the show, that's when we can become aware that we are having an out-of-tune moment. We can only do this from the vantage point of what it feels like to be in tune and connected to our hearts. We have a reference point. Thus we can distinguish between our two basic choices.

This does not happen by understanding the theory. One needs to directly 'experience' the difference. We have to learn to clearly recognize each moment when we are responding from our heads, disconnected from our heart, and each moment when we are in tune, living from our heart. Recognizing this difference can be a challenge.

The ego is expert at maintaining separation in so many ways. The ego can trick us into thinking we are being so very loving, and we might even think that our heart has already opened.

There can be a strong emotional quality that we confuse with the gentleness of True Source's Love. This can be confusing because we have a concept or experience of love and care that we have been conditioned to relate to in our lives. The point is that it is just a concept or version of love and care. We may not realize that this pre-conceived notion can keep us in a box that is based on our past experiences. *The Love of True Source is above any concepts or personal versions that we can have. Are we ready to let go of 'our' concepts and 'our' ways' of loving and caring?*

For example, "I love you so much but you are not listening to what I am saying so that is why I am so angry with you." Or, "If you loved me the way I love you, you would agree with me." These are examples of how our human concept of love has conditions and limitations. We cannot experience True Source's Love through our emotional responses, no matter how strong those responses may be. We can experience True Source's Love through 'feeling' the beautiful qualities in our heart, feelings that are present due to the connection of our heart with True Source. Feeling the natural qualities of our heart, such as peace, joy, and gentleness, is not the same as experiencing emotions created when our head is in charge.

Our ego cannot recognize True Source's Love. People throughout history have said, "God is unconditional Love." The head responds, "Oh, that's really so nice to know", yet our mind is incapable of realizing or experiencing what this really means. *Only our heart can grasp the meaning of unconditional Love.*

Another trap of the ego is to believe we really know or understand about The Love of True Source. When a vessel is full, it cannot receive. If our vessel is full of concepts about The Love, if we think we already know everything about The Love, there is no room for the continuous stream of The Love to flow in us. *We have to stop thinking we know that we know, or, all we will end up knowing is what we already have in our full cup. Being humble is having an empty cup; open to receiving something new, something fresh. An open heart that is humble allows True Source the opportunity to fill it with the most wonderful things. This is why I feel it is important for us to realize this: "I cannot know or do anything better than what True Source's Love can do for me." This is The Love behind all of Creation. If we think we know best, who do we think we are?*

Now is the time for us all to let go of our habit of thinking we know the best way. What served us in other seasons were stepping stones to the season that is upon us. This is the time for us to let The

Love bring us into direct connection with True Source, so that we can be brought Home to our true nature.

What do we want to trust to bring us spiritually Home to who we truly are? Mantras, best intentions, teachers in human form, brilliant intellect or positive thoughts are some of the old ways that may have served us in the past. Now is the time to be open to something new. Only True Source's Love knows the best way.

It is time for us to stop fooling ourselves, thinking, "We know best." It is important for us to realize that we like to do it 'our way' because we are afraid to trust The Love. If we truly trusted The Love, we would not attempt to do it 'our way'. If we trusted The Love, our hearts would be open and all our limitations would be so clear to us.

Doing it our way helps us to avoid our fear of what will happen if we trust The Love completely. And our way is so limited! Yet we hold onto it. Only when our way becomes the way of True Source's Love can our spiritual journey unfold. Our hearts have to recognize this.

When our hearts realize this, we begin to allow The Love of True Source to Love us in a way we have never experienced being loved through human love. Whatever culture, religion or belief system one has, every being is a child of True Source, and True Source's Love is the same for all. The process of true spiritual surrender begins when we allow our hearts to directly feel, enjoy and accept the gentleness of True Source's Love. Only then our spiritual heart will begin to open. It is all about True Source's complete Love for us, and the core of our heart has known this all along.

Chapter 11
The Dangers of a Strong Soul

O ur soul carries the collective memory along with the storehouse of karma from our long journey. The ego of every life we have ever lived is embedded in the consciousness of our soul. This has contributed to the different soul patterns we have carried into this lifetime. For example, if someone has authority issues, it does not mean that the core of those authority issues developed in this present lifetime. Similarly, other emotional patterns and trigger points that seem to be very ingrained in our personality did not just develop over the course of this life. From personal experiences I have had regarding the journey of my soul, I have come to realize that we have all played many roles, from victims to perpetrators, on the different stages we've encountered along the way.

It is important for our heart to realize that we do not exist to grow the stature of our soul. Spiritual growth is the growing of our spirit, our true self, and this happens only when our heart accepts True Source's Love. It is only The Love that can grow our spirit, not our efforts or our doings.

The desire to empower the soul means the ego is still present. The process of empowering the soul strengthens the ego. That drive can take us in different directions, though one thing is for sure: when we live from our ego, we are always moving toward something, but we never seem to arrive. If we do sense that we have arrived, it is only because we have temporarily met a goal. The feeling of fulfillment will be temporary. The drive of ego leads us to the next preoccupation upon our horizon. We want more, better, or different. The next thing will be followed by the next thing, and on and on, until we die.

Each preoccupation gives us a sense of meaning or purpose. It is important to realize that this is the meaning and purpose our ego has chosen to create, but not the meaning and purpose of our spiritual existence. This does not imply that we should not achieve goals in our life. We can use our everyday experiences in life, and the achievements that come along with them, as opportunities to grow the connection between our heart and True Source's Love and Light. Our true purpose and meaning is to always have our heart remain in a spiritual connection; whatever accomplishments or achievements occur in the world are secondary.

Our heart never wants to lose sight of, or feel, the loss of the primary purpose of our existence. The impulsive drive of our ego's attempt to find its idea of happiness will then cease to exist. Only when this happens, will we feel that we have 'arrived', and no longer seek to get somewhere because, in actuality, we have arrived. When our heart accepts True Source's Love, we eventually reach a state where we experience becoming a part of The Love. Knowingly or unknowingly, in the core of everyone's heart, our spark longs to never again be separated from The Source of Love and Light.

The experience of being an instrument of True Source's Love and Light is very different than that of a soul that is radiating and basking in its own glory. When one of us has a very strong soul, we may radiate a charismatic and enchanting quality. Even though this person may say humble things, consciously or unconsciously, a big part of them is very much in love with themselves. Their magnetism can be very enticing and attractive to others who may even place them on a pedestal.

When a soul allows itself to be on the pedestal as a teacher of others, it can be very dangerous because of the illusion of having risen above others. When a soul accepts admiration, devotion or worship energy, then the energy of the soul continues to grow as it is fed by others. Souls such as these can look or seem bigger than life because the radiance of that energy contains a lot of sensation. From that magnetism, they can seem very bright or all knowing and that strong soul may even act that way.

There is an aspect of our being that may admire or be attracted to the magnetism of strong souls. We may even think that this is something good and worth striving to achieve as a personal goal. During our journey through time, we have been playing out the patterns/impulses of our ego during all of our incarnations. The soul is carrying these collective patterns and these soul patterns influence our present life. The strivings of our soul to ascend or to become 'all that it could be' is deeply ingrained because we have followed those impulses for so long. It is time to recognize that we do not exist for the growth of our soul. That in fact, we existed as our true self before we were given a soul. Our soul was given by True Source as a gift to serve as a facility for our true self to awaken. As we learn to choose The Love in every moment our hearts can permanently open. This is how our spirit, our true self, learns to accept The Love so our true nature can be realized. If we do not learn to accept and allow The Love to open our hearts, our spirit will not grow. The reason is that the quality of our non-physical heart mirrors the quality of our spirit which is our true self. This is why it is crucial to realize that the growth of our soul is not the same as spiritual growth (the growth of our spirit).

We do not exist to become, 'I am that I am'. The striving to become 'that' is driven by our soul and not our inner heart. The purpose of our existence is not to become a stronger soul with lots of radiance or magnetism. The Love of True Source is always the most gentle of the gentle and when a person is experiencing being a part of the gentleness of The Love, they may not appear to be as impressive looking as the strong soul appears. When a soul feels, "I am full of light," and view themselves as if they are on a higher dimension, in actuality they are separated from the gentleness of True Source's Love. Souls such as these may have a feeling of aloofness, being above it all, and may even experience a type of intoxication from their perception of how bright they are.

In the name of spirituality, powerful souls often feel they are capable of blessing others and they enjoy owning, or taking credit for the blessings they give. *When we are being an instrument of True Source, we recognize that we are not capable of blessing anyone. All the credit for the blessing is given to True Source. All blessings are experienced as a part of True Source's complete Love for every being. We are simply grateful to be a sweet child of our most beloved Creator.*

When a soul perceives itself as being in an elevated status, it functions as if its existence is a blessing to others. This soul's sense of greatness or higher dimensional status is actually its greatest spiritual hindrance. A soul which is enjoying its elevated perception would probably not agree with this statement because it believes its presence is a blessing and a special gift that it offers the world. What I am sharing can be quite controversial because of the high esteem that many of us hold toward these souls with their elevated status. They may feel inspired to do wonderful things for the planet or for others. Unfortunately, they may not realize their own limitation in regards to the spiritual journey. For example, they may not realize the extent that they perceive themselves as being above others.

I understand that what I just shared is a sensitive issue that may be met with resistance. The reason is because some of you may have a special teacher that you behold with devotional sentiments or might even worship them with all of your adoration. Whether a teacher is alive or already passed, when we have a devotional worship connection with them, we can easily become attached to their form and may not realize the extent to which this becomes a hindrance to our spiritual enfoldment. Based on the direct sacred relationship between the core of our heart and True Source, I felt it is important to share my understanding. I apologize for any discomfort my statements may bring up.

When a being believes they are worthy of receiving worship from others, or they feel they are supposed to receive worship from followers, this is an indication that they are a limited being. True spiritual beings do not accept worship from others. And if a being believes they are benefiting others by accepting their worship, then this is also an expression of their limitation. When the soul of a spiritual teacher experiences itself living in a higher dimension, they may mean well, and feel it is normal to accept worship from others. In addition, they may even think that by accepting worship energy, or devotion from their followers, they are serving the highest good of those devotees. On some level, they exhibit pride; taking credit for their accomplishment, or giving the credit of their greatness to their personal lineage. True Source, the Source of Love and Light and The Source of our true selves, is beyond all lineages and beyond all dimensions.

When someone has a devotional connection to a teacher, the emotional attachment can become very strong. It can be confusing because on one hand they may feel a sense of joy, safety, security and a belief they are spiritually advancing. On the other hand, a deep part of their being may realize that worship directed to a teacher is limiting the fullest awakening of their true self. I consider it to be a great spiritual opportunity when someone begins to recognize that the devotional relationship with their teacher is limiting the most sacred relationship that exists between the direct connection of the core of their heart and True Source. The reason is that they have placed the teacher or Guru in an intermediary role and this becomes an obstacle blocking their direct connection to our Creator. Letting go of this devotional relationship and attachment to the teacher's form can be a great challenge because of the belief that this teacher is the spiritual doorway they had been searching for. From my experience, the only true spiritual doorway Home is The Love of True Source.

When a true self is awakening in The Love of True Source or has become a part of The Love, no aspect of their being is willing or interested in accepting worship energy. All credit is always given to the Perfect and Complete Love of the One and Only Creator. Their hearts realize that to receive worship from others limits them because it interferes with their direct connection to True Source.

From my heart's best understanding, the great messengers from which the world religions are based understood this and wanted us to have a direct connection with our Source. Typically, the religion did not exist when the messenger was on Earth. Over time, followers often misconstrued the deeper spiritual teachings these beings brought. Unfortunately, these misconstructions became dogma or ritual eventually, and a fixation on particular concepts or beliefs arose. Often future followers adhered to those, although this was not what those great messengers intended or would have wished. In my opinion, they wanted our spiritual connection to be experiential, based in the 'here and now', and not a conceptual structure rigidly followed in order to save us at a future time.

In our everyday lives, we come across souls who believe they have a special role to play. This sense of 'specialness' is a big trap. Being a soul that thinks its role is to bestow blessings upon others or grace us with their holy presence is a very different experience compared to the experience our true self has when we allow True Source's Love to open our hearts. As instruments of True Source's Love, we enjoy The Love being shared directly with all beings. Sharing the love is neither about us nor is it happening due to anyone else. Neither is it about our ability, or our belief that we have the authority to bless others. Sharing the love, being an instrument of that Love, is about becoming a part of True Source's complete Love for us and for all beings.

We are not here on Earth to develop the greatness of our soul. That has been our distraction for eons, and it has only gotten us into deep karmic debt. Our soul and physical form were given as a gift from True Source for the purpose of our spirit, our true self, to awaken. This awakening can only happen when we learn to rely on and let The Love open our hearts. As our hearts accept The Love of True Source, our spirit is able to grow. This is why it is referred to as 'spiritual growth'.

True Source gives us our soul and physical form, allowing us to incarnate so that our true self can learn to trust and rely on The Love above all things. When a strong soul continues to grow and believes in the importance of its own radiance, it lives in separation from True Source, and cannot be a team player for True Source's larger purpose. The strong soul enjoys a sense of heightened status, while, simultaneously, the spirit, the true self within the heart, can remain in a contracted state. The bigger the soul plays out its sense of identity on the stage of life, the more the spirit is limited in accepting The Love of True Source.

Powerful souls may say all the right things such as, "We want our followers to grow bright". But perhaps they do not really want them to grow as bright as they are. It is possible that they are coming from a paradigm which posits that they are hierarchically superior and followers are expected to stay on a lower rung of the ladder. They are concerned that their position of greatness may be challenged. In this type of hierarchy, the followers will always remain below.

When the soul is strong, it continues to act like the moon who believes it is the source of the moonlight rather than realizing that all light comes from the sun. This illusion keeps their true self from fulfilling its true nature as a part of True Source's Love. In other words, having a strong soul limits the growth of our spirit. This concept can only be truly realized through direct spiritual experience.

Followers or devotees of a powerful soul can also have their spirit squelched because they are allowing an intermediary to be between the direct connection of their heart and True Source. Unfortunately, this means that in their worship, and consequently within their heart, they direct their love to another being rather than whole-heartedly directing their love and their whole being to the One and Only True Source. The core of our heart realizes that it is our birthright to have a direct connection with our Creator, just as children have the right to have a direct intimate connection with their parents.

When a person lets True Source's Love open their heart more and more, a type of built-in protection comes into play. Since The Love of True Source wants to give us the best, the heart can only keep opening when blockages are dissolved. It is the blockages that we have created that have kept the heart closed. *When The Love of True Source brings us closer to the experience of becoming a part of The Love, then we find that we are not capable of taking credit or ownership. To take credit, we have to separate ourselves from The Love.*

In contrast, *when we experience becoming a part of True Source's Love, we have only gratitude to True Source for all things.*

We are so happy to be instruments, letting True Source's Love and Light effortlessly radiate to the heart of all beings.

When a spirit, a true self, awakens in the gentleness of True Source's Love, it feels so happy when other hearts awaken. Our true self, our true being is not threatened by the spiritual progress of others, because when our spirit awakens in The Love, it is not invested in status, or in reaching a higher level, or establishing a place for itself in the cosmic pecking order. True selves awakening in the gentleness of The Love realize that they are not individuals climbing a mountain to get to a higher place. This journey, this life, is about all of us collectively moving together, and it is not about anybody being above or below another. We realize that all of our spiritual progress had nothing to do with any of our efforts, our doing, our perseverance or our special talents.

Everything we receive and all our spiritual progress is directly due to True Source's complete Love for every being. When our heart realizes this, how could we possibly take credit for anything? All credit is given where credit is due. That is, to our One and Only Creator; our Source of Love and Light and the Source of our true self.

Chapter 12
Emotional Reactivity and the Ego

E motional and mental reactivity are the ego's very good friends because they justify its 'right' to be alive. *The ego has perfected the art of using excuses, and it does so to be able to maintain its stake over what it wants, and to justify reacting the way it reacts. For clarification, in this book I refer to "feelings" as the natural byproducts of our heart, such as peace, joy and love. Emotions are the responses that are activated when our ego is in charge.*

If we are truly interested in spiritual growth, then we have to give up whatever excuses we create that support our emotional reactivity. Our hearts pay a price when we let our ego run the show. Some may say it is my right as a human to express my emotions. As a psychologist, I was trained to assist clients to be able to be in touch with their emotions and to express their emotions. I am not suggesting that we repress emotions.

I understand that emotions are normal from the perspective of being a human. But we are not on Earth to be a human to express the complete range of our emotional experiences. We are here on Earth to learn to become who we really are; to become spiritual beings in a human form.

Our heart is the no drama zone. When we are grounded within our hearts, we are within a sacred space where emotions do not arise as a reaction to our environment. If they do arise, it means we have left the sacred space of our spiritual hearts, and returned to being in our heads, in the realm of ego domination.

Emotions have a purpose if we use them as teachers that help us in recognizing when we are disconnected from The Love. Emotions help to point us to our blockages. They also help us to learn about the ego's patterns and responses, how we let ourselves be triggered by the environment, and what we do in the privacy of our mind. *In the bigger scheme, emotions are meant to help us learn about the spiritual importance of using free will to choose True Source's Love above all things.*

To fulfill our deepest purpose of existence, we have to let go of all our excuses that justify our right to become emotionally reactive. The ego maintains a hidden repertoire of strategies to continue its existence as an independent agent, and these emotional charges allow the ego to stay separate from The Love. Someone may say, "But I have a right to be angry, look at what they said or did to me." In certain situations, such as, for example, a person who was sexually abused as a child, emotions play a vital role for getting that person in touch with their anger, anger which very often is suppressed. However, it is not healthy or helpful if their anger is embellished.

Anger is something to express and then move on to forgiveness, letting go and healing. Some will say, "They do not deserve my forgiveness for the terrible things they did to me."

While forgiveness may be a lengthy process in some cases, from a spiritual perspective, we come to realize that we are the ones suffering from our un-forgiveness. *We may not see it, but our lack of, or unwillingness to forgive others, is related to our resistance to abundantly accepting True Source's Love with complete gratitude.*

The reason is that un-forgiveness toward others has some degree of self-righteousness built into it. That self-righteous attitude is like an umbrella over our heads keeping us from being bathed in The Love. It draws a defensive boundary around us that may seem like a form of protection. We cannot place a boundary between ourselves and The Love of True Source, and still expect to be able to receive and accept the continuous flow of True Source's Love! Our un-forgiveness toward others harms us because it blocks our connection to our Creator.

We may also have other negative emotions, such as unworthiness, guilt, shame, anger and un-forgiveness toward ourselves. If we were to review our ancient past, we would find that we have played out every part in that history - from the most innocent victim to a perpetrator engaging in actions that we never thought, in this life, we were capable of doing. In the long journey since leaving the 'garden', we have performed in the arena of existence in so many different ways. Our soul stores all these blockages, reflecting our ancient past journey. These blockages are not easy to access because they hide in the deepest aspects of our shadow.

Our personality tendencies and the different ways we get triggered are related to these old soul patterns. *Living life has a way of triggering and mirroring our unresolved blockages and issues by bringing them to the surface. That is what life is designed to do, so we can continue to have the opportunity to choose The Love above all things.*

By choosing The Love instead of our right to continue our patterns of emotional reactivity, we allow The Love to dissolve and heal our wounded past. That is why our great teachers appear in those who are best at triggering us emotionally. It is not coincidence that we have the families of origin we were born into. Similarly it is not a coincidence that we are attracted to marry certain people or attract the children born to us. During the initial attraction to the person who becomes our spouse, we may not recognize the extent of the emotional triggers that may soon follow. The attraction is so strong that we follow the urge to marry. Then, after awhile, the honeymoon may be over and we might even think, "Oh, what have I gotten myself into?"

We also attract circumstances into our life to help us learn. Our issues also reflect our blockages. Life brings these issues to the surface so that we have an opportunity to heal and dissolve the block. If we choose instead to allow ourselves to be triggered, old patterns are reinforced, and then we become convinced we have the right to become emotionally reactive. We may think it is okay because we believe we have reasons to react the way we do. Head logic can convince us of all kinds of things.

It is important for us to realize that we are the ones who suffer from our emotional reactivity, because, at that time, we are choosing to be consumed by our ego's agenda over feeling True Source's Love. Our heart has to feel what it means to turn our back on True Source's Love. Whether we want to admit it or not, this is what happens when we follow our emotions, ways and ego habits instead of allowing the Love of True Source to guide us. This explanation is not designed to create guilt, or for you to conclude that we are not doing well enough. The purpose of this explanation is to help our heart realize the proper direction to go for spiritual fulfillment, and to help us to let go of justifying living a life filled with emotional reactivity.

When we choose to allow The Love of True Source to bring us into the depths of our heart, rather than reacting emotionally, we free ourselves from our old patterns of emotional reactivity. As we continue to learn to accept and choose The Love above all things, these patterns can then be cleansed completely, even to the depth of their karmic roots. The Love of True Source always gives us the best. Transcending all Laws, The Love of True Source wants to clean us up and bring us Home, once again, where we can become a part of The Love.

Chapter 13
The Ego Takes Things Personally

If we are honest in reviewing the makeup of our mind, we will see that, when we are living from our head, we have a tendency to be stubborn. Some brains are so stubborn that they refuse to budge. It is like the guy who insisted that drinking a daily bottle of liquor was good for his liver. After his doctor demonstrated that when a worm was dropped into a jar of alcohol it died instantly, the man exclaimed, "See Doc, I knew liquor is good for me, because if I keep drinking, I will never get worms."

When the mind wants to believe something, it will find all kinds of reasons and justifications to hold onto its stubborn perspective.

Unfortunately, people can even justify behavior that is harmful to others. In contrast, our hearts have no interest in control, in competition, or in competing agendas. Heads butt heads. Hearts like to have a 'heart-to-heart'. *When you learn to experience your heart, you realize that your head and heart can look at the same event in very different ways.* When we are in our *heads, we take things so much more personally. We tend to get defensive or protective of our positions. Your heart does not have an interest in taking things personally.* Therefore, when we are in our heart, someone can say something nasty and we are less likely to be negatively affected. We give them permission to have a bad day, or we accept that they have an issue with managing their anger. We can even accept that they just may not like us. We are all free to let our head think and act as if it is the boss; however, if we choose to do so, we miss out on the greatest gift we have while on Earth.

The ego becomes reactive in a variety of ways because its nature is to take things personally.

The reason people react is because their 'buttons' are pushed. They suffer because there is a perception of a personal attack or insult. Very often, when a person is angry, frustrated, or feeling huffy and puffy, they feel comfortable, even empowered, with their emotional expression. Underneath that, they may be feeling hurt, abandoned and/or rejected. All of us have our own version of unresolved issues and it is important that we be gentle with ourselves. From my experience, in the name of spiritual growth, it is easy to become self-critical because we are not as good or disciplined as we think we should be. Yet, that becomes another version of how the ego stays invested and blocks us from our hearts.

Our *heart does not react like the ego does. Why? Because the heart does not take things personally.* If a person gets snippy and says something mean, the heart may say, "Oh, he's really angry right now." There will be minimal or no emotional charge. When the ego experiences the same situation it may say, "How dare they talk to me that way?" We can feel insulted, hurt, and may return angry fire. Or an ego-driven personality may adopt an aloof position of superiority. A well-trained ego knows how to respond without external emotional reactivity. But on some level the ego is affected. It may be hard to see, because the ego is expert at protecting its turf, beliefs or point of view.

When the ego is at the helm of our ship, the energetic blockages and associated emotions are continuously stored in the field of the heart. Some people think that since they did not outwardly express an emotion, it does not count. If we are angry or resentful, and we do not express it to others, the energetic blockage is still stored in the field of our heart.

When we let The Love of True Source bring us into our heart, we can let The Love cleanse the garbage we create from living as an ego- dominant being. There are multiple layers of blockages in our non-physical spiritual heart. These are connected to our soul, which contains the storehouse of karma accumulated from our past journeys. Examples can include patterned emotional responses, revenge, grudge and resentment lists, feeling unforgiving toward others and holding back forgiveness towards our self.

How do we know we are still stuck? We keep reacting. We are not free from our emotional triggers. We have not trusted and allowed The Love to completely set us free. The difference between where we are now and spiritual freedom is that we are stuck in patterns we ourselves created, and we continue to create them blindly when we live with our egos in charge.

We are instilled with the same survival mechanism that animals have. When in danger, an animal will either fight or flee. When a deer is not being threatened or hunted, it will graze peacefully in the here and now. There are times when our lives may be truly threatened and our survival is at risk. But since most of us are not living in an active war zone, our survival mechanisms should not be activated. Yet most people live with at least low-grade activity from their survival mechanisms. That means they do not feel safe and at ease as each moment unfolds. They live in apprehension over the uncertainties in life. To overcome our fears, we attempt to control life according to how we think life should be. When a person feels like they always have to protect themselves and their surroundings, or feel the necessity to be in charge, or feel anxiety over losing control, then their survival mechanisms are amplified. This is extremely draining to their energetic reserves.

The purpose of our life is not to survive. Our purpose is to thrive. Only when our hearts are grateful and open to feeling, enjoying and accepting True Source's Love can we continue to thrive without limit. Are we willing to let go of our 'right' to take things personally? We can choose to hold onto this right, but if we do, with that choice will come a variety of mental and emotional stressors, causing reactions. Even if we have a rationale to justify our reactions, who cares? We are justifying our right to turn away from our connection to the gentleness of True Source's Love in our hearts.

As our heart continues to grow in its realization of what it means to 'turn away from The Love,' we become happy to give up our right to react and take things personally. And what a relief it is to not to have to take things personally! Freedom begins to ring in our hearts.

There is a deep meaning to the expressions, "And The Love shall set you free" and "Love is all you need." The core of our heart realizes what this really means.

Chapter 14
Ego Caring verses Spiritual Caring

O ften in the name of 'caring', we may become angry, outraged, disgruntled or upset with another. But emotional reactivity that claims it is concern for the other is often a deception of the ego. This just adds more negative energy to an already challenging situation. Even if we think this form of 'caring' is helping, in fact our emotional negativity is energetically polluting our hearts, our personal space and the space of those around us.

This is an important realization for our heart. If we are truthful with ourselves, we will realize that the ways in which we emotionally respond are not a true demonstration of care and concern. Let's say one of us becomes very angry from a recent world event. Who is being served by that person's anger or outrage? They certainly are not benefiting from it, and neither is the situation. Becoming arrogant, prideful, overcritical and judgmental are different ways we contribute to the energetic sullying of our immediate environment, almost on a daily basis... And it also contributes to the contamination of our non-physical heart.

Someone else may say, "My friend was just diagnosed with cancer. If I don't show that I am hurt and upset, then it means I don't care." Caring is not supposed to be painful. The highest form of care is not an emotional response. When we are grounded in our heart and our heart is grateful and accepting True Source's Love, then we are best able to love and care for our friend who was just diagnosed with cancer. The Love cannot flow through to our friend if we are tense and nervous. Our friend most likely has enough of his own fear, worry and uncertainty. He does not need any additional fear or distress from us. When we have those feelings, even if we do not say anything, the core of another's heart can sense these non-productive negative emotions.

Our hearts have to realize that the emotional drama often played out in human care is an old ego habit. It does not properly support us or anyone else. When our heart is accepting True Source's Love, then The Love and Light radiates gently and sweetly from the field of our being. The gentleness of True Source's Love can help those around us in so many ways, seen and unseen. Being an instrument of True Source's Love and Light is the highest expression of our caring for others or about events and circumstances.

The same applies with the death of a loved one. From a spiritual perspective, it is best not to grieve for an extended period of time. The way to spiritually care for and support our loved ones who have passed is to allow The Love of True Source to open our hearts so we can be a sweet instrument for our loved one. Calling on them, remaining emotional or asking a medium to communicate with them, while it may make us feel better temporarily, does not serve them in the long run. This can even become a major spiritual hindrance for our loved one. No one would want them to be earth-bound or attached to this dimension. If their 'being' senses distress from their family and friends on Earth, there may be difficulty in disconnecting with the Earth dimension, and this will hold them back on their spiritual journey.

This life was meant to be lived having our whole heart and whole being directed to True Source, accepting and enjoying True Source's Love. This is also what our loved ones who have passed on are wanting as well. If we fail to realize this Love, we miss the real purpose of our incarnation on Earth. By being an instrument for those who have departed, we serve their highest good. Our heart-felt prayers to True Source on their behalf can greatly help them. We can pray from our hearts by asking True Source to help them to let go of everything that is not of The Love, and thus assist them in accepting and embracing True Source's Love and Light with gratitude from wherever they are. To help them on the deepest level, it is important that our prayers be in the gentleness of The Love and not be contaminated with an emotional charge.

When on Earth, if we are well-grounded in our hearts, with gratitude to True Source for all things, then nothing can hold us back after we leave our physical forms. Even if family and friends are grieving continuously for an extended period of time, it will not hold back our soul and true self, which is being directed to The Love and Light of our Creator. In our non-physical form, we are accepting and being embraced by the gentle sweetness of True Source's Love. There is nothing on Earth that can compare with being touched so deeply and sweetly by True Source's Love. We cannot become earth-bound or stuck in-between realms because we have chosen and have made True Source's Love a priority, and that is the most important priority that is available to us to make while still in our bodies. We are truly free when our free will chooses The Love over all other things.

In the past I practiced different systems of meditation. These systems were not based on our heart accepting True Source's Love. During that time I developed several ways to manage the sad news I heard on TV or read in the newspaper. One method was to avoid listening to news and to avoid hearing about the atrocities going on in the world. Another method was to assume a 'rising above it' attitude I acquired from the type of meditation practices I was doing. I considered all this to be spiritual and a form of self-care. There was a quality of detachment and aloofness I cultivated in order to not be affected by negative events. This approach helped me to not be emotionally attached to negative circumstances. The problem was, that being detached, being aloof, I was not being an instrument for the highest good for such a circumstance.

Today however, my reaction to negative events is different. When I hear of an atrocity going on in the world, I remain connected to True Source's Love, and feel The Love radiating from my spiritual heart. My experience, along with others I know who are letting The Love open their spiritual hearts, is that when we hear bad news, our heart actually opens bigger and The Love radiates more gently and sweetly. The reason is that when we exist to be an instrument, The Love of True Source radiates more and more to places and people in need. This is an expression of 'spiritual caring'. All humans on Earth, as well as other beings on all dimensions, are in need of our spiritual care. Most likely this is different from our old version of caring, which may have been tinted with human emotion and limited human understanding of what True Love is.

It is important for us to be grateful for the opportunity to let True Source's Love and Light touch the heart of every being. Spiritual caring is the same as being an instrument, and this spiritual caring becomes the natural attitude of our heart when we begin to let The Love set our heart free.

Chapter 15
The Illusion of Protection

If someone is very angry at us, and we respond with anger, we may say, "I have a right to get angry and return fire." This is a typical way in which our egos react. However, from a spiritual perspective, this is not the best way to respond. When grounded in our hearts, we can be firm when firmness is called for. We can also be in our heart while engaging in assertive communication even while interacting with someone who is being verbally aggressive toward us.

We may think we are benefiting or protecting ourselves by emotionally fighting fire with fire, but in fact, we are engaging in a type of psychic warfare. When we return fire with anger, we become more vulnerable to the negative energy being sent our way. The reason is that darkness resonates with darkness. *Darkness cannot exist in light.* This is why darkness disappears when you turn on the light in a dark room. Darkness cannot penetrate into a field of light.

When we remain grounded in our heart by trusting, feeling, enjoying and accepting True Source's Love, then The Love and Light that radiates from our heart becomes a wonderful, beautiful, and protective cushion. Dark energies from the environment are not able to penetrate into the gentleness of The Love radiating from our hearts.

In contrast, when we return anger to someone who is angry at us, whether expressed or not, a non-physical connection is created with the other person and with their anger. It is like a toxic psychic cord that carries the exchange of the negative energies flowing back and forth. So, when we choose to hold onto our right to be angry, or we remain furious at someone for years to come, we are the ones that suffer. The back-and-forth toxic exchange of anger between two people becomes detrimental to their physical health and hinders their spiritual growth. This is why letting True Source's Love help us to forgive everyone for everything is so important and cannot be avoided for our spiritual growth.

What we may not realize is that our un-forgiveness towards others is related to our un-forgiveness towards ourselves, and fosters our resistance to accepting True Source's complete Love for us. Through the connection of our hearts to True Source, we can let The Love help us to forgive those who have hurt us by their words, thoughts, behaviors or their emotional reactions. When we forgive from our heart, the negative psychic cords are dissolved. Anger toward others ceases to be. Very often, when we feel wronged by another, we may think we have already totally forgiven them. On a cognitive level we may think we have forgiven them because we have said, "I forgive you". But, at the level of our non-physical heart, the resentments are still there and continue to build up over an extended period of time. They can be there even without our consciously being aware of them. We can use Open Heart Meditation to let True Source's Love help us to forgive everyone who hurt us in any way and to cleanse the stored negativities from the layers of our heart. An internet link for a free download of the Open Heart Meditation by Irmansyah Effendi is provided at the end of the book.

When we choose to let The Love help us to let go and heal our resentments, on some level, the other person often changes for the better. The reason is that we have chosen to end the dysfunctional dance. Our heart is now much freer to open to The Love. We find great joy in being an instrument toward those who had previously been on our resentment list or on our extreme dislike list. Many painful relationships are healed. For example, during an Open Heart Workshop, one participant shared that her brother refused to have anything to do with her. They had not spoken in over two years. After forgiving her brother through Open Heart Meditation and smiling to his heart, within a day the brother called on the phone. The door was now open for the two of them to heal their pain and value their relationship in a new way.

Many times, a healing like this does not take place until one of them is on the deathbed. Then, one of them says, "I am sorry for staying away from you for so long." Whatever healing needs to take place on the deathbed should not wait until one has two days to live. Now is the time to remove all the resentments, unresolved issues or blockages toward anybody anywhere that you may have. Even though some of us may think it is our right to hold onto our anger or resentments, it does not serve us. It is another way the ego keeps the real you separated from True Source's Love.

It is so easy for us to put up defensive boundaries because we may be scared of getting hurt or taken advantage of. Yes, it is true that people can be mean, and people do hateful things to one another. We may have been hurt from the past. But creating and keeping a defensive armor does not fix that, nor does it protect us. As explained before, we are more vulnerable because the defensive posturing closes us off from The Love and Light. Blocking The Love and Light is when we are most negatively at risk.

Our hearts have to realize the illusion of thinking we can protect ourselves by hiding, staying separate and closed. It may seem safe, but it is an illusion. Hiding, being armored, keeps us locked in a cocoon. Our hearts have to realize that the presence of True Source's Love is unconditional, so gently and sweetly welcoming us in every moment. There is nothing to fear, ever, because True Source never judges us and never wants us to suffer. True Source's Love wants to give us the best of the best in each moment. It is we who are not accepting The Love. True Source is not capable of hurting us because the nature of The Love is to Love. Why would we want to stay in separation and deny True Source from doing what True Source always wants to do?

It is time for us to begin opening to the experience of letting True Source Love us completely and continuously. This is what True Source wants to do so that all the wandering children in the desert can be brought Home to the joy of our true nature. *And by feeling, enjoying and accepting True Source's Love with gratitude, we can then be instruments for True Source's Love to radiate to the hearts of all beings on all dimensions, everywhere. It is important for our heart to remember that this is the number one assignment we all share and the bigger purpose of why we exist on Earth. When we are in True Source's Love and Light, there is no need to be concerned about defending or protecting ourselves. Relying upon the Love and letting The Love bring us into our hearts is the safest place to be.*

Chapter 16
The Pecking Order and the Ego

When the ego is in charge, there is a tendency to create a sense of a pecking order. When animals do this we call it jockeying for position in the herd. If you reflect back to your upbringing, you might remember how these pecking order patterns played out in the neighborhood and schoolyard. In its meanest and crudest form, this takes the shape of deep and ugly prejudice and a warped justification for treating people as less than human. History demonstrates that all throughout time humans have been repeating these patterns. In its more subtle form, jockeying for position in life can be seen when we become arrogant, putting others down or finding fault in them. If we do this, it is a clear indication that we are in our head and not grounded in our heart.

Our heart has no interest in putting people down or judging them because the core of our heart knows that every human being is our sibling. The gift of our heart allows us to be patient and tolerant of imperfections in others in a way in which our head does not. Some may say, "If a person is out of line and our heart does not see it or react and judge them, then we may end up a sucker and be taken advantage of." But, in fact, the heart can see clearly what is happening, yet not react. Being in the heart means we can see more clearly because we can respond without emotional reactivity or judgment. This does not mean that we have to agree with the behavior of others or that we are a 'push-over'. From the heart, we hold our ground and communicate firmly whatever is called for. If you are a boss, it may mean having to fire someone because of violating company rules. However, having to fire someone when you are grounded in your heart is a much different experience than doing it when the ego is in charge. And even though the person may not like getting fired, they will most often appreciate the heart over the ego-style approach.

Sometimes we may be condescending, attempting to put others on a step below us. By finding fault with others it allows us to feel more secure in our own position. If we are honest with ourselves, we realize that we have played this ego game on a number of occasions in our life. It gives us a false sense of security or worthiness. One gets to think they are more worthy because they have placed others below them. We do this when we judge each other.

By finding fault in other people, it also helps us to feel more secure in our own sense of who we think we are. This pattern that the ego plays so well is linked to feelings of arrogance, righteousness or superiority. Egos like company to support their position, so they might associate with a group that has similar beliefs about the lower status of another group, race or religion. This is why scapegoats are so popular. History has shown us the dangerous pattern that has occurred over and over again when one group scapegoats another.

Families create scapegoats, identifying one person who is viewed as the problem in the family. Often a child's acting out is a cry for help within the dysfunction of the family's dynamics. In our neighborhoods and schools, scapegoats are commonly formed so groups can have someone they can view as being below them or less than they are. Even professionals often have a tendency to place others in the field below them. For example, brain surgeons may view themselves as superior to family physicians or some psychologists may view themselves above a clinical social worker. An M.D. may not view a dentist as being a real doctor. Egos have a natural affinity for pecking orders. The term "climbing the corporate ladder" reflects the games egos play to get ahead as they strive for more and more power.

The nature of the ego is to compare, but not all egos do this in the same way. Another version of comparing is when the ego views itself as less than others. The ego accepts a role of being lower on the pecking order, with primary feelings of insecurity and inadequacy showing themselves in slumped physical posture and self-critical statements. When the ego accepts its role as being lower on the pecking order, we run the risk of attracting abusive relationships. For example, we may attract a spouse who is verbally abusive and frequently puts us down. This allows our ego to confirm its inadequacy as it experiences being a victim. One part of us may say, "You have no right to treat me that way," but another part of them is saying, "Yes, I am getting what I deserve because I really am not good or worthy."

Sometimes we can play both sides, as we fluctuate from feeling superior or above others in one moment, and in the next moment we may feel not good enough or less than others. Wow! The games our egos can play are capable of taking us through an assortment of scenarios. The play of the pecking order can often be heard during intimate relationships. I can remember when I first got married, and I kept thinking my wife was trying to control me. What was interesting was that she was feeling the same thing about me. Our egos would rebel and say, "You are not my boss". Now that we are able to enjoy a wonderful connection between the core of our hearts and True Source's Love, the dynamics of our relationship flow so much more smoothly. We do not get triggered the way we used to because we are more patient and accepting of our differences.

One thing is for sure. When the ego is in charge, it always finds a way to maintain its right to exert its concept of freedom, wanting to be an independent agent that is separate from The Love. This is not true freedom. This is an illusion of freedom.

When we live from our heart, we are in a stable space, and we don't have to judge or compare ourselves to others. We can still form opinions, though our opinions do not have the emotional charge or arrogant flavor that is associated with judgments. From the perspective of our heart, we do not view or relate to life in terms of a pecking order. If we do find ourselves playing the comparing game, defining ourselves as being more than or less than another, it is an indication that we floated up from our hearts into a head, ego-dominant space. When we are grounded in our hearts, we remain in direct connection with True Source's Love flowing through our hearts. When we no longer feel a need to seek a position in life by comparing ourselves to others, we come to the experience of equality. Our heart allows us to have the recognition that every being is our sibling, that we are all equal, because we are all children of True Source.

There are people who may try to insult us, who see us as their enemy, or perhaps they are just in an obnoxious mood. But this does not change the fact that beyond the veil of their limitation, the spark of Love and Light is in their heart. When some of us live dark lives, the spark can become very dim; however, even these beings are still our spiritual siblings because we are all children of True Source.

Our egos may stubbornly say, "My enemies or evil people do not deserve the right to be forgiven." Our hearts say, "True Source, whoever I used to dislike or think was my enemy, please let Your Love bless them more and more and give them the best of the best." Our heart knows we are all a big family. Well...in the past, honestly, it's been quite a dysfunctional family. Now, as more of us are instruments, allowing True Source's Love to radiate sweetly and freely, then more and more of our hearts awaken in The Love.

It is time for our hearts to realize what it means for us to have the blessed opportunity to be instruments of True Source's Love and Light. Then our life will be used for the bigger purpose of why we truly exist.

Chapter 17
Scorecards and the Ego

The ego likes scorecards so it can keep track of when it thinks we won or lost. The problem is that the purpose of life is not about winning or losing. The ego will keep us thinking that at any given moment, we are either getting ahead or getting behind. But, what it thinks of as ahead is not true progress. No matter how 'ahead' we get, for sure it means that our 'head' is in charge. 'Ahead' can mean getting a promotion, a new house, a new car, paying off bills, etc. This does not mean that we should not accomplish wonderful things in the world. A good job, nice surroundings and secure finances are wonderful, but there has to be a realization that this is not spiritual progress. These are examples of worldly success. We exist to 'experience' spiritual progress. Our everyday life is meant to be the vehicle for our spiritual growth.

Yet, too often, we lose scope of this because the ego views progress and success from its own standards. The ego is tricky and can convince us that we are growing spiritually or making God happy by following our religious beliefs. There is a tendency to think we are growing spiritually when we do what we think are good things such as helping others, doing good deeds, or standing up for a cause. Helping others is so wonderful and important, but very often it is our ego keeping score of doing good deeds. Our good deeds are performed when the head is dominant. The ego assures itself that it is doing the correct things in life. The problem is that if we do good things to keep score while our head is in charge, then we do not receive any spiritual benefit. Instead, our ego gets to put a star on its scorecard and say, "Way to go, 'I' did well." The ego thinks it is achieving something very worthwhile, according to the method of comparison it has created.

For example, the comparison may be, "I am doing more and better than I did before," or "I am doing more than they are," or "I am doing more and more of what I am supposed to be doing." *When* the ego meets the standard it has set, it convinces itself it is making progress, and therefore declares, "I am good enough." When the ego fails to meet the standard it had created, the ego feels it is not being good enough.

On the scorecard of the ego, there are lots of pluses and minuses, all on the same day. This is based on the system of how the ego is judging itself and its performance. According to the methods of comparison and the standards the ego determines to be truth, we have a variety of human experiences. In the life of an ego, the methods and standards of comparison can keep changing. *The ego keeps thinking what it sees and experiences in the world is real, but in actuality it is only a self-created projection. The ego can also think it is progressing spiritually or that it is saved because of its self-created belief system. It believes what it believes and therefore it is so.*

This is why belief can be such a trap. *A belief can simply be a mental construct that allows the ego to feel secure in its ways, its likes and dislikes.* It can be very convenient for us to accept that a particular belief we have has saved us for all time. Then we get to assume that everything is going to be all right. *The spiritual journey is not about "everything is all right" according to the ego's concept of truth.* It is not about believing our heart is in the right place. The ego may have a sense of progressing and moving forward as if it is getting closer to the top of the mountain. It may think it has reached the top of a mountain or is at least approaching the apex. Our ego may achieve a great score on its personal score card according to the definition of spiritual growth that it has formed.

True spiritual growth has nothing to do with our personal score card, or how well we think we are doing, and it is not related to all the wonderful things we have done. True spiritual growth lies far beyond the ego's opinions of whether or not we hold the correct beliefs, understanding or a grand sounding philosophy. Nor does our spiritual growth have anything to do with convincing ourselves that we have the right answers and the correct approach.

It is time for us to let go of our scorecards. The true spiritual journey is not about how good we can become. It is about our trusting and accepting The Love of True Source above all things, with abundant gratitude, each and every moment of our lives. This means we are willing to let The Love help us to let go of all our judgments toward ourselves and toward others. *True spiritual progress can only be measured according to the quality, openness and condition of our heart and how well our hearts radiate The Love to the world.*

It is easy for us to get enticed into bathing and basking in the glory of our soul's radiance and to then think that we are progressing. Learning to feel, to trust, to enjoy and accept The Love of True Source while allowing The Love to open our hearts more and more, means we are making true spiritual progress, getting closer to our Creator.

Allowing The Love to dissolve all our blockages that are not a part of The Love, means we are making real spiritual progress. Only True Source's Love can grow our spirit or true self. Growing our spirit, our true self is what spiritual evolution is all about and the reason why we truly exist. With this understanding in our hearts, we can become instruments for all beings according to the way of The Love.

Chapter 18
The Ego's Use of Arrogance

Another device the ego uses is arrogance. When we are getting disturbed or critical because we know we are right and another person is wrong, then that is a gift, letting us know that the ego is in charge and our heart is closed. Another example of this is thinking people should see things our way. This is at the core of many conflicts that occur in relationships. When we experience friction during a conversation it's because we believe it's not okay for others to disagree with us. We think others are supposed to see the world or our position the way we do. It is common for our ego to react and not allow another's view to be different than ours. When we do this, it is another signal letting us know our head is dominant, and in that moment, we have the opportunity to shift out of the attachment to our personal agenda and into our heart.

The reason it is so easy for us to get into power struggles is because our egos seek 'I am right and you are wrong' solutions. This does not mean that we should stop sharing our points of view with others. It means that we share our point of view from our hearts instead of our heads. When we express our views from our heads, there is a good chance we will do so with some attachment to the outcome. We want others to see it our way, and if they do not, then it can trigger an emotional response along with an arrogant attitude.

When we have arrogance and think we are right, being right gets us a step up the illusionary ladder that leads to nowhere. Due to our arrogance, any step upward that an ego takes to be above another person, is a spiritual hindrance. Whether we are right or wrong is not the point and does not matter.

Arrogance and pride are major obstacles that can be very subtle to recognize. Our heart does not have to agree with another's viewpoint. When we allow The Love of True Source to bring us into our hearts, we do not get into power struggles, even if the other person is trying to pull us into a dysfunctional dynamic. Our heart is loving, not attached to being right and gives others permission to be different. Accepting differences in this way leads to healthier and more fulfilling relationships.

Again, accepting differences does not mean you have to agree with their position. Just the act of accepting someone's right to be different helps to create a more loving and supportive environment. Even if it appears that they have an irrational perspective, they will then feel safer and more open to consider our point of view. When someone can feel our acceptance instead of our disapproval, it gives them a potential freedom to let go of their attachment to their position. They do not have to hold on so tightly to defend their turf. If they sense that our ego is judging them, there is a good chance that they will hold onto their position more emphatically, because a fear of losing their right to independence has been triggered. Accepting differences also leads to greater understanding. Accepting differences is a gift that our heart offers us for creating positive relationships and helps us to remain open to deeper realizations about the bigger picture. These gifts provide the opportunity for heart–to–heart communication instead of a head-to-head battle.

Heart-felt acceptance of our differences with others allows us to be respectful in our disagreements. It gives people space to be who they are, just as we like to be given the space to be who we are. If we remember a time in the past when someone attempted to take that space away from us, we may recall that we became rebellious. Similarly, others feel rebellious if we take away their right to think what they want to think. When our heart is open, we do not get rebellious because The Love that opens our hearts connects us to The Source of Love and Light. When we get emotionally triggered because someone is insisting we see things their way, it signals that we have entered into a head-to-head battle. Our arrogance and pride kick in when we feel offended, and we are judging them just as they are judging us.

There is a saying, "Misery loves company". When an ego is in an extremely unsettled place, it is in a state of misery. Sometimes the ego will want to push people's buttons and pull them into a drama. What the drama is about may not matter. They just want to butt heads and create drama. Then they do not have to be alone in their misery. If we are getting pulled into the drama, the ego can sense it. It knows it because it can sense our buttons are being pushed. Our anger or frustration becomes the food to feed the fire of the drama that continues to grow. At this point, their emotions are also feeding the fire of our emotional reactivity. The dance can go on for an extended period of time, even if we are not in the same location. This is another example of how resentments and unresolved emotional blockages contaminate the field of our heart.

How do we transform this kind of ego-driven psychic attack? If someone is attempting to overpower us with their words or trying to trigger an emotional response, and we choose to let The Love keep us grounded in our hearts, then we feel The Love within our hearts and do not enter into the drama. When this happens, sometimes the person's emotions and attempts to pull us into the drama will become amplified. However, after some time their resistance will be deflated because we are being an instrument for them. They are being softened by the gentleness of True Source's Love radiating from our hearts. Our heart is not judging them for their imperfections and emotional reactivity. When we are properly in our heart, our own or another's arrogance is a non-issue because we have chosen to be grateful for the gentleness of The Love.

It is important for us to learn to recognize the varied expressions arrogance can take as it easily slips into our everyday interactions, or dances in the privacy of our thoughts. These moments are cues to let us know we are not grounded in our spiritual hearts.

Chapter 19
Excuses, Excuses, Excuses

Excuses are one of the favorite foods for our ego. Excuses allow the ego to maintain its identity as a separated being that has the right to be angry, resentful, outraged, hurt, insecure, judgmental or aloof. It is often convenient to blame someone or something else for reasons why things in a given moment are not as good as they should be. This is a way we often use excuses to shift responsibility away from ourselves.

Excuses can also be used as a means to justify our right to withhold positive feelings toward others. This is ironic in that we are the ones who always suffer from holding back positive feelings. The different excuses for why we think we have a right to be emotionally reactive occur in so many shapes and forms. If we sincerely want to grow spiritually, we have to be willing to give up our excuses and justifications regarding our right to all of our emotional reactions.

This is not an easy concept or process for us to accept. Sometimes we hold onto our repertoire of ongoing excuses as if it were a matter of life or death. *We may not realize the extent to which we are determined to hold on to our sense of entitlement to exert our personal will. To give up our right to use excuses feels threatening to the ego, because if we give up our excuses, our ego will lose a significant amount of power to maintain itself as a separate and reactive being.*

For example a person may say, "I am angry because he did that to me. If only he had not done that, I would not be angry." We have an excuse or reason to justify why we should personally be offended. Our excuses also provide us the justification to judge and blame. *When we choose our heart by feeling and accepting True Source's Love, we can be relaxed, peaceful and balanced in moments when we would have previously had our anger or other emotions triggered. We can smile and have no desire, no inkling, to judge or blame others, blaming them for our feeling or having negative emotions.*

Many of us have read in spiritual books about the importance of non-judgment and how our judgments of others are really a reflection on or judgment of ourselves. Even our head may agree with the concept that we have no right to judge anybody for anything, still, we go ahead and do it anyway.

Before following the way of the heart, I reached a point where I had to be honest with myself. I had the philosophy that it was wrong to judge, that I had no right to judge anybody for any reason. Though I realized this, I was constantly going against my philosophy. I was constantly judging myself and others. I knew it was wrong, but I did it anyway, because my head was dominant and the ego was in charge of the show. *The ego finds it natural to judge and does so in both obvious and very subtle ways. The ways can seem so natural, that it can be difficult to recognize how frequently we are actually judging people or circumstances in our everyday lives. Judgment disguises itself in what we have come to think is normal, so we keep doing it over and over again without even realizing we are doing it.*

When we judge, arrogance or the illusion of spiritual superiority is not far around the corner. When we are truly in our heart, our heart does not judge because it is not capable or interested in doing so. It is important to note that disagreeing with someone's poor choices is not the same as judging them. When we disagree without judgment, we do not create any emotional charge or sense of superiority. We do not have the feeling of being above or below another and we simply let them be. As I shared before, this does not mean we are not firm when firmness is called for, though we are able to execute firmness while allowing The Love to keep us connected to our heart.

When we let True Source's Love open our spiritual heart, we can enjoy our heart while giving the world permission to be imperfect. And, it is important to realize that we all have imperfections. Many times our words, thoughts and actions do not support the highest good of others. When we allow our ego to become emotionally reactive and play out the subsequent judgment or blame that follows, we are also being imperfect.

The ego is so tricky because it deflects, providing excuses or reasons for why it is not our fault. The ego can act as if it is a total victim and fail to take ownership for the role it may have played. This creates a victim versus villain dynamic. For example, we may feel "I am the victim and you are the villain." The other person may feel that *you* are the villain and they are the victim. This dance is commonly played out in intimate relationships. The ego defends its right to be right along with a justification to judge others as being wrong. The ego does not play fair because it's capable of judging people for the same behaviors or traits we may have. For example, we may react with arrogance to someone else's self-righteousness or get mad at them for expressing their anger.

Just as we want to be accepted with our imperfections, it is important that we allow space and room for others to be imperfect. When we are letting True Source's Love bring us deep into our hearts, not only do we not judge them, we let True Source's Love radiate freely to give them the best. When friends, family or co-workers are playing out their weaknesses, rather than getting triggered into our old ego patterns of emotional reactivity, we smile and can be instruments for them. We do not judge or become offended. *Our ego takes things so personally, while our hearts can be very patient with the imperfections of others. Close relationships are our wonderful training grounds because they provide excellent opportunities for our unresolved patterns to surface.*

How we respond when people do things we do not like or agree with is a mirror into ourselves. Any person or thing that pushes our buttons in any shape or form becomes our teacher or a facility for our spiritual growth. When we experience judgment, blame, or any expression of emotional reactivity, rather than focusing on the external trigger, it is important for us to recognize that we have resistance somewhere in our being. Rather than realizing that the key issue is the friction and that the resistance is within us, we tend to stay focused on the external trigger. Then, with our emotions on the trigger, we think we have a good excuse and reason to remain in a state of emotional reactivity.

Excuses, excuses, excuses. We are the ones who suffer from our excuses because we end up choosing and defending our right to be offended. Every moment we do this is a moment in which we turn our back on True Source's Love. Our heart has to realize what it means, what the consequence is, when we choose our excuses and related emotions over our heart's connection to True Source's Love.

This precious gift of life provides opportunities for our patterns to surface so we can learn to choose The Love above all things. When we feel, accept and enjoy the gentleness of True Source's Love, our blockages and ego patterns dissolve and our spiritual hearts begin to open more and more. Learning to choose True Source's Love above everything else is why we exist on Earth. This is the process of how our spirit, our true self, awakens and grows to become a part of True Source's Love.

Chapter 20
The Ego's Perception of What It Needs

Many of us are aware of our ego's drive. Some will feel driven but they are not sure what direction they are heading. Others feel driven and are heading in a clear direction towards their goals. Just because we are driven and achieve what we seek does not mean we are truly successful. As previously explained, we are here for spiritual success, which is directly related to the opening of our spiritual heart. To obtain great worldly success while failing to experience opening the spiritual heart, is to lead a misdirected life that fails to hear the deep call of our inner self.

Some of us have souls that are so inflated, that we may act or feel like deities in human form. Our sense of personal power and greatness can override any fear associated with the survival mechanism. We live more with a feeling of invincibility because of the elevated state we think we have achieved.

As previously explained, we do not exist for soul empowerment. *Our true purpose is not about what we can achieve, create, manifest, or how we can use our intention to influence life. Our soul and physical form are gifts meant to serve as a vehicle so we can take form on Earth for the purpose of our spiritual development. The purpose of the soul is not to exist for its own purpose, but for the soul to be a facility for fulfilling our spiritual destiny. Who we really are is not our soul. The essence of who we are, the spark of our true being that lives within the heart, is our spirit, our true self. Only when our heart accepts True Source's Love, can our heart open and grow. As our hearts open more and more, our spirit begins to shine and our true self awakens from its long slumber. It is only then that our true self is actually on its way Home, fulfilling the purpose, the true nature, of this life.* Spiritual growth is meant to be an effortless joy. It becomes easier and easier as we learn to gratefully trust, feel, and accept True Source's Love. Then True Source's Love naturally brings our spirit closer to our original and true Home.

Knowingly or unknowingly, we are all in the process of evolving from being head-centered and ego-dominant to being heart-centered. One of the blockages that keep us preoccupied and stuck in our mind is our perception of what we need. In actuality, to exist on Earth we need air, food, water and shelter. If our needs are not met we shift into survival mode. Yet, our tendency is to relate to our desires, hopes, and expectations as if they are needs. When we say, "I need this," or "I need that to happen," this need of ours is a self-created illusion, not a real need. The aspect of our being that says, "I want," is often a hidden need in disguise. Our heart realizes that our desires, hopes, and expectations are mental creations that keep us preoccupied, busy with living for the purpose of getting what we want to get out of life.

Pursuing and fulfilling our desires and expectations reinforces our pattern of being an independent agent wandering through the universe with our own agenda. An aspect of us may say, "Of course I have the right to create and get what I want from my life." *With this approach, we will exist and live selfishly, just for us. We will not choose or feel the need to exist and live for the bigger plan...the plan that invites us to be an instrument of Love and Light, radiating The Love and Light sweetly and freely to the hearts of all beings in the whole existence.*

It is not necessary to live from the position of our desires, hopes and expectations. By remaining in connection to True Source's Love, our hearts feel true joy, and True Source gives us the best of the best, and everything takes care of itself in a wonderful flow and rhythm. We plan and respond to the moment, doing so without the ego, the mind, creating needs, desires, hopes and expectations.

When you are grounded in your heart and feel the gentle sweet connection to True Source's Love and Light, then trust grows, as you experience how everything unfolds within the Will of the Divine. If what you choose to plan does not happen, then you trust that it is not within True Source's Will. You move on without any emotional reaction. *When we are driven by self-created needs, desires, hopes and expectations then, if they are not fulfilled, we end up with disappointments or emotional reactions. If they are fulfilled, we end up with a stronger more-powerful ego and soul. Life becomes a rollercoaster with ups and downs driven by whether our desires, hopes and expectations are being fulfilled or not. We will live as a head chasing rainbows beyond our reach. We will fail to live our life from our heart, as a spiritual being in a human body.*

If we find ourselves thinking our wants are needs, or we find ourselves driven by our desires and hopes, then this confirms that our head is in charge. Our mental perception of a need is totally different from the perspective of our heart. Our heart does not relate to life from the view of needs and desires. *Our heart is simple, and knows that what we truly need is just to be in connection with the Source of Love, which is the Source of our being. To our spiritual heart, this is true joy. When we allow our heart to continuously accept The Love of True Source with gratitude, the thirst in our being is fulfilled by the eternal well that never goes dry. We do not thirst for the desires of the world. When we are living our life from the identification of ego consciousness, then there is a part of us that is continually dissatisfied, that becomes bored with whatever we achieve and will always feel lack. It is like a thirst that cannot be quenched.*

We may jump and chase one need or goal after another, and another, to the next, but where does this lead us? It creates an illusion that we are progressing forward as we move through time. Are we really progressing in our life? As shared before, success and progress in life are not based on what we achieve. It is determined by the extent to which you learn to trust, feel, enjoy and accept The Love of True Source. When your heart allows you to accept True Source's Love, your heart opens bigger and bigger, your spirit or true self grows, and you move closer and closer to our true Home, and to fulfilling the true purpose of your existence.

We are here on Earth to bridge the gap between our state of isolated independence and the joyful experience of becoming a part of The Love. Let us learn to really appreciate and value True Source's Love, in the same way that we recognize, appreciate and value clean air, water and food that sustain our physical being. The core of our hearts never wants to be separated from The Love. *Instead of being driven by our ego, our lives are being called to joyfully experience the gentle and sweet longing of our hearts to reunite with our Creator.*

Choosing The Love is not something we do by being the 'doer' in charge of getting closer to our concept of spiritual perfection. *We have to realize that for so long we have been relying on 'us' as being the key, and really, if we are honest, we are still unhappy and still searching for happiness. Relying on us has never, nor will it ever work. Now is the time to properly learn to use our spiritual heart; to feel, embrace, accept, trust and rely on True Source's Love. Until we accept our own limitation to spiritually progress, we will not be able to allow The Love to help us so that we can receive the best of the best.* When we learn to let The Love help our heart to feel, our heart naturally follows the feeling and trust grows. Naturally, we then find ourselves relying more and more on True Source's Love and our spiritual connection deepens.

As we begin to accept and enjoy The Love, choosing The Love above all things, we will begin to see life through different eyes. In addition to experiencing an inner calm, peace, light and joy, there will be a growing feeling of being loved completely. That is something beyond our mind's capacity to comprehend! We are here on Earth to become who we truly are, to become a spiritual being who enjoys the beauty of consciously living as a child of the Creator.

Chapter 21
Letting The Love Have its Way

My first intimate experience with death occurred when I was fourteen years old. My father had a heart attack at my house and while giving him mouth to mouth resuscitation, I experienced him take his last breath on Earth. I was not mature enough at that time, and neither did I have the proper guidance from others, to transmute this event into a meaningful learning experience. It was a shocking experience and I had a lot of confusing emotions that I found difficult to share with others.

When I was twenty-two years old, I found myself sitting with a family on the side of the Bagmati River in the Himalayas of Nepal, whose brother had died. We watched their loved one cremated on the stack of wood that had been recently piled. At that young age there was still a part of me that felt invincible. As we all stared into the fire, it seemed as if time had stopped while we watched the physical form of their loved one become a burning corpse and then be reduced to ash. It was a deeply sobering remembrance of the impermanence of this world. That flesh, which not long ago pulsated with life, was now residual ash that the family literally swept into the flowing river.

When we relate to the things of this Earth as if they are permanent, we fail to realize the temporary nature of all things.... including our possessions, our relationships and our physical form. *Only The Love of True Source is permanent. Whether or not we realize it, The Love of True Source is our life line and our refuge in the ocean of existence. True Source is the only Perfect One and The Love of True Source is the only Perfect Love. In order to be brought closer to True Source, our Creator and Source of our true self, our spirit, our spark, we must allow The Love to have its way with us.*

The Love can only have its way with us when we let The Love bring us into our hearts. When we remain head-centered, even as a mindful observer of our thoughts or emotions, The Love cannot do what The Love wants to do...and that is to remove the blockages that keep us separated from True Source's Love and Light. We believe that it is much better to be detached and observe our ego patterns rather than play them out. But while mindfully observing our consciousness can create a calmer mind, we still exist separated from our spiritual heart. This is what many of us have done on our spiritual paths.

The nature of The Love is to dissolve everything that is not of The Love, so that The Love can set our hearts free.

The observer of our consciousness has to submerge into the spiritual heart for us to be fully present as a heart. This happens when we let go of our ability to observe and allow True Source's Love to bring us into our hearts. Being within the heart properly, The Love can then begin to help and guide us to become proper instruments of The Love and Light for every heart in existence.

These days, so many of us are talking about the importance of the heart. We know that our heart is the key to spiritual fulfillment. The problem is that when we do spiritual practices that involve our perfecting a technique, we are the 'doer' in charge of getting results. We may think we are connected to our hearts but one thing is for sure: if we are the ones who are in charge of doing a technique, then we are not truly in our spiritual heart. The reason is that only True Source's Love can bring us into our heart and this can only happen when we stop relying on 'our' ways and techniques, and begin to rely on The Love. *If we do not rely directly on True Source's Love, then we become dependent on how good we think we can become.*

When I was in the Himalayas, in Nepal in 1975, I lived and studied a comprehensive yogic system with an old yogic monk. Back then, the big achievement was to quiet the monkey mind. The old monk referred to the mind as a drunken monkey that likes to jump from branch to branch. There were different practices we did daily which focused on breathing techniques (pranayam), yoga postures, trying to cleanse and open the main energy centers (chakras) and on awakening the kundalini. We ate a pure vegetarian diet and fasted frequently. In meditation practice, the focus was on the higher energy centers. I spent many days meditating eight hours and sometimes more. After being able to experience the space between my thoughts and the space in between my breaths, I felt I had reached a place of being 'above it all.' At least I felt that way while I was meditating. I thought I had found the way. I thought I had found everything I was looking for. All I had to do was keep meditating with discipline, commitment and perseverance. I believed that through this approach, my mind would be purified and I was on my way to enlightenment.

I intensely practiced this particular system of meditation for 11 years before I started questioning it, and finally I was willing to admit to myself that something was missing. I had a 'rising above it all' feeling and I believed that I was growing spiritually but my unresolved issues began to become very obvious. I started to realize that I was 'bypassing my stuff.'

The 'stuff' I am referring to is the soul's stored accumulation of karmic blockages from our past journeys which are reflected in the layers of our non-physical heart. My wake-up call came after the birth of my first son in 1986. He was born with severe colic and was up for many nights, and my wife and I were sleep deprived. Once, in the middle of the night he would not stop crying and I felt this intense anger come over me. I just wanted to pick him up and throw him! Of course I did not do that. But I began to question the spiritual path I had followed for so many years. At this time, I was also in the middle of my Doctorate in Counseling Psychology program at Florida State University, and I was teaching meditation and stress management workshops. I began to realize that focusing on the higher chakras was able to give me the sense that I was growing spiritually but, in actuality, I was bypassing my deepest blockages. In the meditation that I was doing, my soul was growing in stature, and this is what gave me the feeling of spiritual growth.

It began to make sense to me why many of the yogic monks, and many of the advanced spiritual teachers or Gurus I had met over the years, talked about their experience of rising above it all, yet were often emotionally reactive. It appeared to me that in their meditation, they were 'rising above it all' through a process that bypassed their 'stuff', 'stuff' which they may have even denied existed. It was obvious to me that the deeper heart was not being cleansed. The original cause for their negativity was not being addressed. I remember seeing patterns of arrogance, spiritual superiority, and anger in the advanced teachers that were supposed to have risen above the mundane world. When the spiritual heart is not cleansed, the heart does not open properly and our spirit or true self remains in confinement. The soul may continue to grow in stature from meditation practices but that is not the same as spiritual growth. *If we do not allow The Love to open our hearts, our true self does not awaken in the spirit of Love and Light.* Some of us may have the most impressive, powerful and magnanimous soul, but as the power of the soul grows, simultaneously our spirit is squelched. *A powerful soul and a true self awakening in the sweet gentleness of True Source's Love cannot simultaneously exist. This is why many paths may seem as if they are helping us to spiritually grow, but they may be leading us down the very limited path of soul development.*

Regarding mindfulness practices, I agree that it may be better to observe the patterns of our mind as they surface from our unconsciousness and not be attached to these patterns, rather than let our ego play out its agenda. But just observing our patterns is a limited approach compared to letting The Love completely cleanse these patterns. Is it not time for us to let The Love have its way so that these patterns, residing in the deep layers of our non-physical heart, can be dissolved forever?

From my heart's best understanding, I have come to realize that experiencing spiritual fulfillment is not about practicing our way, or how perfect we can become, or what level of self-mastery we can achieve. It is simply about letting The Love have its way. The only way for spiritual fulfillment to truly happen is for us to give up the illusion that achieving it is up to us. How we have used our free will throughout the long journey of our soul is reflected in the multiple layers of blockages stored in our non-physical hearts.

The law of cause and effect is the law of karma. Every time 'we' act as the doer, every time we use our free will, we create karma. The seeds or imprints of our actions, our karmas, are stored in our heart and soul and, as they accumulate over time, they become blockages in the heart. It is the accumulation of these blockages that keep us from allowing True Source's Love and Light to radiate to the hearts of all beings.

Every time we experience a negative emotion, the negative emotions get stored as seeds in our heart and soul. When these seeds ripen, we reap or suffer the consequence, or fruit, of our actions. This is the meaning of the saying that, "What goes around comes around" or "As you sow, so shall you reap." Karma is meant to serve us, by providing lessons to teach us. These lessons teach us that when our ego is running the show, we are out of alignment with our deepest spiritual connection. These energetic blockages or karmas develop when our ego's desires and drive lead us astray. We have wandered down dead-end streets, sometimes getting caught in a maze of seeking name, fame, and power, just to fulfill the ego's excessive needs or desires. Our ego creates excuses to justify the righteousness of our behavior. So many times our thoughts, emotional reactions, and our behaviors have not been in alignment with our highest good. In our journey through time, we chose to react in ways which were completely different from how we would have responded if we had let True Source's Love connect us with our hearts. If we are honest with ourselves, we may realize that this is true even in our present life.

Reflecting on our past journey, we see that all the suffering we have experienced was caused from the heart blockages we created from using our free will. Elevating our sense of consciousness by connecting to higher energy centers does not remove the multiple layers of karmic blockages our souls carry or the multiple karmic blockages that our hearts are filled with. Traditionally, yogic systems based on controlling the breath, on awakening the kundalini, specific mantras, and meditating on the higher chakras were designed to speed up the ripening and clearing away of one's karma. When we meditate using these techniques, our meditation practice accelerates the ripening of our past karmic seeds. Being the 'doer' in our meditation practice amplifies this process, and can cause the seeds of our past karma to ripen more quickly.

We are meant to learn from our suffering. Most likely we do not even realize the extent to which we are suffering right at this moment. *Living separated from True Source's Love as an independent being with our ego in charge is the most extreme type of suffering. We only begin to realize this when we let True Source's Love bring us into the depth of our hearts. Then when we leave our hearts and return to our ego's domain, we feel the pain of separation, and we realize the pain of separation has enslaved and kept us in prison. Yet we have acclimated to the state of separation, of suffering, and have come to view it as our normality.*

The Law of Karma is a gift from True Source to help us learn to choose True Source's Way and True Source's Love above our ego's ways and the drive of our soul. It is through this learning process that our spirit, our true self, is awakened and grows to become a part of True Source's Love. Only then can we come Home to who we truly are.

What happens when we choose to rely on True Source's Love? True Source's Love is above the law of karma, and The Love does not want us to suffer. We may not realize what a Blessing this is. What does it mean that True Source's Love is above the law of karma? It means that when we let The Love bring us into our hearts, *then The Love effortlessly dissolves all our karmic seeds and all our deep inner blockages. We experience no karmic suffering, because the seeds of our karmas from the long journey of our soul are dissolved and will never have the opportunity to ripen. When we rely on the Love and let Love be the doer, we stop creating more blockages or seeds of karma in the soul and the heart. We simply let The Love remove that which is keeping us separated from The Love so that we can spiritually grow and fulfill our true nature, our true purpose.*

Beliefs are mental constructs. Some religions have a belief system that says, "I have been forgiven and all my sins have been washed away." This is only true to the extent to which we allow True Source's Love to penetrate into the multiple layers of our heart to cleanse and dissolve everything that is not of The Love. The only thing that is supposed to be in our heart is the radiance of True Source's Love and Light. All our karmas, or 'sins,' are energy blockages we accumulate when we live as an ego stuck in our heads and separated from The Love. Simply having the thought, or believing in any savior, does not dissolve the accumulation of all blockages. This type of belief only comforts the mind. Someone believing may feel assured that death will result in a permanent place in heaven. *Salvation is only salvation when the heart is completely free. Just because we believe our heart is free does not mean that all issues and blockages are dissolved. Our thoughts, words, and actions reflect the quality of our heart, and the quality of our heart says it all.*

The extent to which we have no issues with anyone, anywhere, on any dimension reflects the extent to which our heart is free, free to allow for the gentleness of True Source's Love to radiate. The radiation of True Source's Love then flows sweetly and freely to the heart of every being in the whole existence without any resistance. Until then, we still have karma or what may be understood as the 'sin' of separation from Love. Even if we don't think we have any issues that 'thinking' does not mean we are free. It is very easy to fool ourselves on this because our blockages and issues can be subtle and find tricky ways to hide from The Love.

We do not realize the different ways and the extent to which we are attached to our concepts and habits. In so many different scenarios we use our old ways so that we can continue to be 'us' and feel justified in our ego's choices. For example, this is how we justify our right to become arrogant, angry, greedy or self-righteous. We are afraid to lose our identity, our 'me,' and have convinced ourselves that we know what 'me' is. The part of us that fears True Source's complete Love is afraid because it thinks if we let "Love have its way"...our 'me' will be destroyed. Our ego has frantically been calling,

"What about me!"

The irony is that the 'me' we know has never been who we really are in the first place. The reality is that we have been defending and protecting at all costs 'who we are not', laboring under the illusion that we have been protecting who we are. We have forgotten the truth of who we really are, that we are sparks of Love from the Source of Love and Light. Failing to realize the blockages we have created, we continue to protect our right to be 'who we think we are.' And this has blinded us to who we truly are. We are the children of True Source.

It is our being within our hearts, feeling, and following the feeling of enjoying and accepting of True Source's Love with gratitude, that takes care of everything for us and begins the process of cleansing whatever is in the way of letting The Love flow freely. This is similar to a mother who wants to clean her child who has been playing in the mud. The best way for our spiritual heart to open is to be like a child, welcoming The Love of True Source, letting True Source, our True Mother, wash away all the mud so our hearts can be clean and our blockages can start to dissolve.

We are where we are today because of the accumulated history of how we chose to use our free will in the past. *The opening of our spiritual heart is an ongoing process. The condition and quality of our heart is a reflection of our spirit, our true self. Our spirit, our true self, grows by embracing and accepting The Love and Light of True Source. This is how spiritual growth happens.*

All of our experiences on Earth are blessed opportunities for our blockages to surface so that we can learn to choose True Source's Love to dissolve them for us. This is what spiritual growth is about. If our unhealed patterns surface and we do not choose The Love, then the patterns are further ingrained and reinforced. This manifests in many ways; how easily we can get triggered in our everyday lives and habits, which keep us separated from The Love. Living from our heart is so important because when we allow The Love to bring us into our hearts, we do not get pulled into our old patterns.

When we follow our old ways, we continue to strengthen our separation from The Love. Our ego becomes stronger and stronger. The use of our free will to do things according to our wants, hopes and desires continues to spin a karmic web around us. Of course, True Source has complete Love for every being, and The Love is always present waiting to give us the best. In the core of our hearts, we know that it is time for us to come into alignment with the bigger picture. The great plan is to become instruments of True Source and to enjoy, with abundant gratitude, the gentleness of The Love radiating to the hearts of all beings. Is it not time for us to let The Love have its Way, so we can fulfill the purpose of our existence?

Chapter 22
Being Grounded in Our Hearts

It is important to feel well-grounded in life. Many of us are aware of this. Having a healthy, energetic connection with the Earth is important for our physical health. Without having a proper ground-connection to Earth, our bodies are not able to maintain healthy balance. Aspects of our energetic system will be overcharged while other aspects of our system will be depleted. As a result, physical impairments can occur. Using another metaphor, the yin and yang in our energetic field will not be balanced.

Some meditation practices focus on the cultivation of the energy center a little below the navel. This is often referred to as the lower *dan tien* in Chinese or the *hara* in Japanese practices. People can even learn to perform impressive physical feats from cultivating their *hara*, though this is not to be confused with spiritual evolution. *Tai chi* and *qigong* primarily work with the *hara* or *dan tien* energy center. These types of practices, using the breath and a meditative focus, can help one experience a sense of balance and harmony, flow and rhythm. People may feel that they are tuning into a vast storehouse of energy because they attune to the larger *chi* energy field maintaining the energetic flow of all of nature. In the 1990's I practiced and taught these kinds of modalities. There are positive health benefits. It is very easy for one to feel the magnetic quality of energy and to experience how intention and the breath are able to circulate *chi* in our energy body. Personally, I came to feel that it was like eating ice cream but the ice cream had no sweet flavor. Circulating the chi felt very impersonal. There was energy, balance and power, but it was missing the connection to the gentle sweetness of True Source's Love.

In cultivating energy, one is also at risk of getting overcharged in such a way that the soul, personal will and ego become very strong. I could feel that happening in my being as I got deeper into advanced

Taoist internal cultivation practices. Tuning into the internal *chi* field led to the awareness of a greater *chi* field, but sensing this is not the same feeling as coming home to the sweetness of True Source's Love, which is beyond any experience of energy.

Although balance and harmony with nature are helpful in our lives, they do not automatically lead to spiritual growth. Spirituality is not about how balanced and harmonious with nature one can feel. It is about our willingness to feel, accept and enjoy True Source's Love with gratitude, letting The Love gently bring us into deeper and deeper levels of the heart, so that our hearts can open bigger and become brighter. This is how our true self awakens, by relying on the gentleness of The Love. If the soul grows stronger, building the power in the energy center connected to our navel, this additional strength in the soul interferes with the opening of our spiritual heart. We can let The Love open our heart and simultaneously be energetically well-grounded to the Earth. In terms of spiritual growth, allowing The Love to connect us to the Source of Love and Light is the best and safest way.

As we open deeper to The Love, we feel True Source's Love flow through our hearts to the core of the Earth. Being an instrument for the Earth is very beautiful. Rather than simply being a host in a body, on the Earth, we get to share The Love with all of nature's formations. We realize that the Earth is a living being and what a great blessing it is for us to have the opportunity to be on this Earth dimension. Relying on The Love, allowing The Love to do it for us, is a totally different experience when compared to grounding by being the 'doer', imagining or visualizing that we are in charge of cultivating or directing energy.

For spiritual growth, being well-grounded and rooted in our heart and not in our mind is most important. The key to this is to not be pushed or pulled by inner or outer influences that distract us, leading us away from our heart connection. We are in the process of a spiritual evolution that calls us to new and deeper realizations and to true grounding in The Love. If we are rigid, we will get stuck in our old ways and patterns. We miss the call. Perceived storms from the world will come and go. They are an inevitable part of life. They are the gifts of challenge that continue to appear as opportunities, inviting us to surrender to the great plan... and the plan is where we get to choose to accept True Source's complete Love above all things. Challenges in life help to strengthen us so that we can become more and more grounded in our hearts, no matter what our circumstances are.

People will always be doing disappointing things, acting out of ignorance under the domination of the ego. While our mind may judge and react, our hearts forgive people and grant the world permission to be imperfect. This is very important, because in reality, people act in imperfect ways. Our judgment of others hurts us and dirties our heart. *Focusing on the imperfections of others creates resistance in our being and along with states of strong emotional reactivity, reinforces the experience of maintaining our separateness from True Source.* The more subtle expressions of this may be difficult to recognize because the feelings of aloofness, judgment and arrogance can become so normal that they feel like our second nature.

Our primary and true nature is to enjoy with gratitude the gentle radiance of True Source's Love. But our true nature, which resides in the core of our hearts, is being squelched by the dominating patterns of our heads. As we learn to be grounded in our hearts, our true heart nature, our joy and gratitude, become as real and as natural as breathing.

The perceptions and realizations of our heart are completely opposite from those of the head. Our heart accepts that we are all works in process, and that everyone is our sibling, and that what matters most above all things to our heart is accepting the gentle and sweet Love of True Source in every moment. Being grounded in True Source's Love, *we can be grounded in our spiritual heart, and grounded to the Earth all at the same time. This is the path and the alignment needed to become a proper instrument for the Earth and for all beings, even during the moments when our eyes are open.*

It is time for our path to be lit not by our soul's sense of radiance or good intentions, but by the direct connection of our heart to True Source: the Source of Love and Light, our Creator, and the Source of our true selves.

Chapter 23
What Will You Rely On?

The ego can be quite convincing in getting us to believe what it wants us to believe, even when proof is introduced that says otherwise. The ego has a way of forming four walls that are designed from a particular belief system it finds useful. These four walls, or four directions, are then used as a compass to help guide or navigate the way in which the ego moves. The ego becomes comfortable sitting in the box it has created and is resistant to change. It becomes so invested in its belief and approach to life that this becomes its truth and reality. The ego is unable to see beyond the four walls it has created.

It is similar to the man who went to the doctor because he was convinced that he was dead. The doctor said, "You are standing here before me breathing and talking, so there is no way you can be dead." The man insisted and said, "Doc, I don't care what you say, I know I am dead." The doctor asked, "Do dead men bleed?" The man said of course not. The doctor took his sterilized needle, poked the tip of his index finger and squeezed out two drops of blood. The man replied, "Doc, I was wrong. Dead men do bleed." The man who believed he was dead was shown proof that he was alive, but he stubbornly chose to hold on to his belief.

This man's behavior may sound silly but this behavior is very similar to what we often do when we are dominated by our ego. We can believe something to be true, so we keep believing it, and sometimes without question. If something comes along and challenges that belief, even though the shortcomings of the belief are exposed, we may continue to believe it anyway and hold onto it for dear life.

There is an old expression in America, "Don't talk about religion or politics." This advice has been passed down for generations because people realize religion and politics are very sensitive issues. The reason is, that religious or spiritual notions and how we approach our spiritual journey are directly related to the beliefs that built our 'box', the meaning we give to life, to our relationship to God, and how we seek and perceive enlightenment. Something that challenges our spiritual beliefs is often met with resistance. I can understand that many of the concepts and approaches shared in this book may challenge your personal spiritual belief systems. And I am aware that this may invoke disagreement. Even though this may invoke controversy, my heart is guiding me, telling me that now is the time to be frank and share what I know to be so about True Source's complete Love for every being.

One of the major themes in this book is that our spiritual approach boils down to one of two choices. Choice number one is that you can rely on yourself, on anyone, or anything else that is not in direct connection to The Source of Love and Light. Relying on yourself includes you being the 'doer', you being in charge, responsible for your spiritual progress, which is achieved through your commitment, determination and effort. You are at point A and spiritual achievement is at point B and it is up to you to get there by doing something. This includes relying on any meditation techniques to bring you to your goal. It also includes placing a living spiritual being, such as a Guru, saint or highly acclaimed teacher, in an intermediary position above you. The same applies to placing an angel, ascended master, or a great being no longer in physical form as an intermediary between your heart and True Source. This means that on some level you are counting on them, depending on them, to make everything better in your life and on your spiritual journey. By placing anyone in this hierarchical position, you are placing a being in between the direct connection of your heart and the Source of Love and Light, your Creator.

I am not suggesting that we should not have great teachers that we deeply respect. This is not about our respecting them, but about the position in which we hold them. Spiritual teachers are meant to be like good coaches cheering you on to have your own direct connection between the core of your heart and True Source. It is best if we do not place them in the middle between True Source and our heart, because then our worship energy ends up going to them and not directly to True Source. When we die, and pass from our physical bodies, our heart and soul may still be directed to the teacher or being in the middle. This slows the journey of our spirit/true self Home because we cannot properly accept True Source's Direct Love when our heart is directed to another being.

The sense of devotion we give to a Guru or spiritual leader can activate emotional feelings, and as human beings, we can feel extremely loyal to them. A type of psychological transference occurs and we may start acting like we want approval from our 'daddy', the one who is going to save us. *The problem is that when we give another being our love and our power and place them in an intermediary position, we limit our spirit, our true self. This does not serve us. It does not allow the core of our heart to have a direct connection with our Creator, our One and Only True Parent.*

How would you feel if your child was not able to have a direct connection with you, his parent? If he had to go through his brother to get to you, that would most likely seem odd. You may say, "My child has a right to have direct access to me." *A healthy parent naturally wants their children to have direct personal access to them. So it is with True Source. True Source is waiting for us to let go of our old ways and habits, inviting us to have a direct connection to True Source's Love. The Love is always waiting but never compelling or forcing because The Love is gentler than gentle and softer than soft.* This is a very important realization for our hearts. True Source is calling and waiting for us to trust The Love so we can have a direct connection with our Beloved Parent.

True Source has complete Love for you, me, and for everyone, and that is our birthright, the right of every spark, to have direct access to this Divine Connection. To settle for anything less is missing what is most important in the whole of existence. Existence was created to facilitate our heart getting back into a direct connection with our Creator so our spirit can fully awaken. It is easy for us to fool ourselves into thinking that there is some other purpose for our existence, and something else more important than True Source's complete Love for every being.

Our opportunity to feel, enjoy, trust and accept True Source's Love with gratitude, so that The Love can dissolve everything that is not of The Love, is precious. This is the proper and only way in which we truly grow spiritually. This is the essence of what this book is about. Now is the time for us to allow the lid of the box our ego has created to be opened, the walls to melt, and for us to let The Love have its way with us. Our conscious or unconscious belief structures that involve our being in charge, our getting anywhere spiritually by being the 'doer', can be viewed as misguided at best, as arrogant at worst. Arrogant when, for example, we become grandiose in what we believe we can spiritually accomplish by our efforts. Remember, this is all being shared within the light of what The Creator, the Source of our true self, The Source of all of existence has to offer us and is always offering us. True Source wants nothing more than to Love us completely every moment and beyond forever.

My son told me when he was five years old, "Dad, I can drive the car myself to the other side of Earth." He believed it and his belief was very real, even plausible to him. As a parent, we can see how ridiculous this belief is. It is just as ridiculous to continue thinking that, "I know the best way to achieve enlightenment and I have the right to choose my way." All this 'I' is, is our ego, and all it does is create further separation.

When we begin to rely on True Source's Love above all things, not as a belief system but as a direct experience felt within our spiritual heart, our spiritual awakening accelerates at a phenomenal rate. As I stated before, this can be a very big challenge for some of us. For a long time, we may have been practicing our spiritual path in a specific way. In that approach, we were in charge, striving to perfect ourselves, striving to get closer to our perceived goal. *Letting go of what we have been following can be scary because those things have become a part of our identity and what we have held to be reality and truth.* I am so grateful that I was able to come to the realization that my spiritual journey was limited by what I alone could do. In all the years that I was in charge, I could only go so far by my own doing. Although the different systems of meditation I practiced assisted me in having experiences I never had before, they stopped short of providing me a tangible direct connection with True Source that can only be established by relying on The Love above all else.

I remember when I took my first workshop with the Padmacahaya Foundation. I was feeling some frustration with my limitations and progress. There was a woman in the workshop who had never meditated before. Perhaps, she may have never read a spiritual book. Yet, I felt her heart was radiating so sweetly with True Source's Love, and here, with all my training and practice, I could not feel what she was feeling. I said to myself, "This isn't fair! I spent nearly three years in the Himalayas and have spent thousands of hours in meditation and she has never meditated before." What I did not realize at the time was that I brought 'my way' into the process. I was being the 'doer' in charge of meditating. She did not know how to do anything, so it was easier for her to let go and just let her heart feel, enjoy and accept True Source's Love without significant interference from her mind's participation.

Thirty years of meditation training did not help me experience my heart on a deep level because I had developed strong habits related to being the witness and observer of my process. I used to think of my witnessing ability as my great strength and friend. Now I realized that all it had strengthened was my personal will, my ability to be a 'doer' in charge of using 'my intention.' Even though the focus, commitment and perseverance I had developed meditating over the years helped me to enter into the stillness in my mind, I now realized that my effort was blocking me from trusting The Love of True Source.

As I now teach Open Heart Workshops, I find the biggest obstacle to feeling the love within the heart is the tendency of participants to practice their old ways and habits of doing things. They try, observe, look or expect, and these actions or habits limit them, and keep them from experiencing their hearts on a deeper level. If they are open to letting go of their old ways, then The Love gently removes their limitations. Most people can learn to feel and enjoy their hearts very easily. What a great arrangement. *The more we feel, enjoy and accept True Source's Love, the more The Love opens our spiritual heart. For me, this is the best deal going in existence. It is the best win-win arrangement! The less you do and the more you enjoy, the more trust begins to grow, and naturally, without any effort, True Source's Love begins to gently radiate, and all hearts gain great benefit. By feeling and enjoying The Love, you get to be an instrument of The Love and Light, so that your primary assignment on Earth can begin to be fulfilled.* One of the most important questions you can ask yourself is, "What am I relying on?" We exist to learn to rely on The Love of True Source above all things and for all things. True spiritual growth can only occur to the extent that we learn to rely on The Love in every moment instead of relying on 'our ways.'

Chapter 24
The Gift of Heart Intelligence

When we open our hearts, we get to utilize the gift of heart intelligence. This is the innate loving wisdom of our heart. *Heart intelligence guides us to make wise choices. It helps us to learn lessons that we were failing to learn when we were stuck in our heads and falling into the same old holes. Heart intelligence helps us to perceive the bigger picture and develop greater clarity about situations and relationships. In contrast, head intelligence,* the perceptions of our mind, is often very limited. Heart intelligence gives us new perspectives, insights and realizations about people, situations and events. It is the best connection to rely upon for whatever challenges come up in our daily lives.

Due to the ego-based consciousness of human beings, societies create rules, regulations and laws to keep people in check. If a person is living with an open heart, they do not have to be taught the Ten Commandments. Their heart knows the most appropriate action in any given moment.

When True Source's Love radiating through our heart is strong, we will cringe at the idea of doing something that goes against our heart intelligence. But if the head is dominant, there is a chance that the ego can figure out a way to justify its actions. Even though the excuse or reason may be ridiculous, the ego is capable of believing it in order to act on behalf of its self-interests. Our head can make poor choices and lead us astray. That is why many of us in the past may have experienced, "I knew in my heart I shouldn't have done that, but I did it anyway."

Following the heart can be tricky because sometimes we may think we are following our heart when we are really following our emotions. When we are truly grounded in our heart, we are experiencing the gentleness of True Source's Love. This allows us to be in the position to make choices without an overlay of emotion.

When emotions arise along with our hopes, desires and expectations, then we are not in a position to experience the wisdom of our hearts. Even though we think we are making a heart-centered choice, we may be making an emotional choice because our emotions have been activated. This is why we make poor choices and blame our hearts when actually we are making an emotional choice. Experiencing the gentleness of True Source's Love radiating from our hearts is the best way to help us realize when our emotions might have been activated and clouding our perceptions.

There is nothing wrong with using an analytic process to help with decision making. But the problem is that the analytical approach is brain-based and the brain, the mind, only provides us a limited view. The intelligence of our heart takes into account the bigger picture, and the roles that each of us play in our connection to the whole. Having heart intelligence allows us to step out of the world of our personal box, to see in a neutral way the dynamics of the surrounding space. Some of us have experienced this. The conclusions and problem solving solutions we come up with when our head is in charge are very limited. We realized this after we let The Love and Light of True Source bring us into our hearts. When we were in our hearts, we experienced a totally different perspective and understanding of the situation. We were able to get in touch with creative solutions and had the heart wisdom to approach problems, relationships or circumstances in a completely different way.

When we live with an open heart, remaining connected to our experience of True Source's Love, using our heart intelligence becomes a natural part of everyday life. It guides us to say what is important at a given moment and to keep our mouth shut at other times. When the field of the heart is strong, you may be just about to say something, and your heart will invite you to keep quiet. Or you may not want to say something, and you will feel your heart telling you to speak. The more we are able to remain grounded in The Love radiating from our hearts, the easier it is to effortlessly enjoy each moment. If something happens and you feel yourself being pulled out of your heart and into ego domination, it will feel painful. This pain is a good sign. It means The Love radiating from your heart does not want you to leave. When you begin to become ego-dominant, The Love pulls you back into The Love, because the nature of True Source's Love is that it never wants us to be separate from The Love. As our hearts become stronger from our deepening connection to True Source's Love, we effortlessly live in that sacred space. It becomes our nature.

By becoming stronger, I do not mean having stronger sensations. When referring to the heart as being strong, I mean that we are in the gentleness and sweetness of The Love. When the heart is getting stronger, the gentleness and sweetness of Love becomes more and more sublime. We are being embraced by The Love and feel we are becoming a part of The Love. We find ourselves effortlessly in our heart, enjoying the gentleness of The Love.

This does not just include the times you are sitting with closed eyes in meditation or prayer. You can remain in gratitude for True Source's complete Love for every being even while you are engaging in your everyday life. Whether you are doing the dishes, driving your car, waiting in line in the supermarket, it does not matter. You are able to experience the gift of the moment in whatever you are doing, because in that moment, your heart is experiencing being Loved. Your heart is expressing gratitude for True Source's Love for all beings. This effortlessly happens as you live your daily life and the gentleness of True Source's Love remains as an ongoing presence.

The deepest experience of heart intelligence is the realization of our inner heart, which resides within the spiritual heart and is the very core, the essence of our true self. Since the inner heart is the direct spark of Love and Light from the Source of Love and Light, it is the only part of us that is completely pure. To feel the inner heart is to remember, to feel our longing to be reunited with True Source's Love. Our hearts understand that when we know something from the "core of our heart," it is a deep realization in our being. Our inner heart holds the connection to our deepest truth. Our inner heart holds the memories, the remembrance of our spirit, our true self, before we separated and left our true spiritual Home... before existence was even created.

Everyone has an inner heart but not every spark, not every true self is radiating. Some sparks are a dim glow or a flicker of a flame, perhaps because they succumbed to worshipping fame and power instead of True Source's Love. Their heart and soul blockages may be extensive and dark like storm clouds. Unfortunately, they may only be invested in getting more fame and more power out of life. Their self-centered attempts for increased power are a mistaken search for happiness. They are our confused siblings looking for fulfillment in the wrong places. All along, they fail to realize that heart is the key to their greatest treasure. Yet, no matter how power seeking someone may be, their heart is always waiting to be free. It is important that we not judge others for their limited behavior, because in our journey through time, we may have acted in ways in which we would now consider unscrupulous.

The deepest intelligence of our heart is always ready to guide us as we learn to rely on True Source's Love instead of our own ego's agenda. True Source is always waiting, always inviting us to open our spiritual hearts. It is time for us to let The Love do what The Love wants to do.

Now is the time for us to allow our heart intelligence to guide our lives so we can make wise choices in each moment. Without heart intelligence we cannot grow spiritually because we will continue to make poor choices that are ego-based. Heart intelligence supports the opening of our spiritual hearts.

Chapter 25
Open Hearts Set Healthy Human Boundaries

Boundaries can be defined as the quality of interpersonal space we create with a person. Boundaries are not fixed. Therefore, there is a dance of boundaries that takes place in all relationships. Boundaries are capable of changing from moment to moment based on the type and quality of the interaction we are having. There are two extremes of unhealthy boundaries: enmeshed boundaries and disengaged boundaries. When the ego is dominant, there is a tendency to be pulled toward either of these two extremes.

Enmeshed boundaries are when our presence, our energy field, becomes entangled with another person's energy field. An example of this is when we are triggered by another person's responses or even simply by their presence. Any little thing they do or say annoys us. If we let this happen, we are responding to life as if we are victims being triggered by the imperfections of others.

When caring about someone or something becomes painful, this is also a sign of enmeshed boundaries. Our attachments to people create enmeshment. In our relationships, when we develop attachments to our expectations, our ego feels it has a right to the outcome we expect. When our expectations are not met, friction is created. The ego is also capable of developing different degrees of possessiveness. When an ego is experiencing possessiveness, in a way we can say it is 'possessed' by the other person. Then, if this person we 'possess' does not fit into the expectations our ego has created, the ego feels threatened, abandoned or rejected.

At any given time, if someone is feeling enmeshed or entangled in their boundaries with us, it is as if they consciously or unconsciously attempt to trespass into our space. If we allow ourselves to emotionally react, they succeed and enter our space. Simultaneously, we trespass into their space. The point is that, the only way someone can trespass into our energetic space is, if we allow them to. When our head reacts and our emotions get triggered, we open the door and flash a big sign that says, 'please trespass here'. We then allow the vibration of others to become entangled in our space. In a sense, we have allowed ourselves to be invaded.

While enmeshed boundaries are more of a hot response, *disengaged boundaries* are more of a frigid response. We go into a state of disconnect and shut ourselves off. We detach, but in a cold way. We form disengaged boundaries when we may be feeling overloaded, fearful or hurt. Disconnecting is a type of defense. Someone can say something and we ignore everything that is being said. We create a state of isolation and do not realize our ego is causing this lonely distress.

There can also be a lot of aloofness when an ego disengages and acts as if it is above it all. From the perspective of mental health, disengaged boundaries can be a time-out, because in certain situations if a person feels they are going to blow a fuse, they withdraw from the situation. When they respond by pulling away, it can be better than becoming enraged or causing harm. Sometimes we can disengage from the world because we need a break. We shut off our cell phone, do not check our emails for a couple of days, and relax. That type of disengagement from the world is important to do from time to time.

However, most often disengagement is non-productive to our spiritual growth. When we disengage from others we cut ourselves off from our hearts, and often our head identifies with our patterns of aloofness, arrogance or pride. It is important for us to realize when we are doing this, because it is a clear indication that we are not in our hearts. *No matter what anybody has done, every human is our sibling. If we ever look down at someone for any reason, arrogance and pride are not far away. This does not mean we have to approve of everyone's actions. This is more in reference to our attitude toward them.* If you see an alcoholic on the side of the road asking for money, you may or may not give them some money. What is important to note is whether or not we disengage and go into a judgmental or aloof space. We are meant to remain grounded in our hearts with the realization that we are equally all children of True Source. No one is above us or below us, nor should caring about other people be painful or overwhelming. Remember, if it is painful, most likely we are head centered. Being heart centered with healthy boundaries, we express our caring joyfully as an instrument of True Source's Love and Light.

It is common for two people expressing human love to do a dance between enmeshed and disengaged boundaries. For example, one minute they become so reactive that they feel emotionally on fire. The next minute they are disengaged and frigid toward one another, fearful that they are losing control. In a sense they are competing for control. One person is saying, "You are trying to control me." The other person says, "No, you've got it all wrong, you are trying to control me." They have lost themselves in the relationship. Then they are either scared because of feeling out of control or angry because they feel the other person is trying to control them. As a result, they withdraw into a disengaged space. They may act cold and respond as if they didn't care. There is a saying, "I can't live with you and I can't live without you." This is how the dance of boundaries can play out. The person feels pain from separating from their mate, and their attachments pull them back into the dance. Some are capable of switching back and forth quite quickly between being enmeshed and disengaged.

Our friends and families are a gift to show us the quality of our boundaries. They become a mirror for us. We get to see the different dances the ego plays as demonstrated by our unresolved issues and patterns of emotional reactivity. Our interaction with friends, family, workplace, and life provide the opportunity for our own limited patterns to come to the surface.

Psychology teaches about having healthy boundaries and communication styles. For sure, this is an improvement over bouncing between the extremes of enmeshed and disengaged boundaries. But from a spiritual perspective, the goal is not to have a healthy ego. *Our biggest lesson from our interactions on Earth is to learn to choose The Love of True Source over putting our attention on creating healthy boundaries or a healthy ego. Then we can learn to remain grounded in our heart under all circumstances. When our hearts are open, we naturally and effortlessly maintain healthy boundaries. We are able to accept differences, tolerate the imperfections of others, and not get pulled into drama. When a situation calls for us to be firm, we do so in a respectful way. We do it from a natural, heart-centered, neutral space that is free from judgment or charged emotional responses.*

When we are grounded in our hearts, we can still disagree and see limitations in others, but we do not harbor condemnation or arrogance regarding other people's weaknesses. The core of our heart feels love, and realizes that every heart in the whole existence is our spiritual sibling. We are all part of a process that has been going on longer than our concept of time can comprehend. Instead of judging, our hearts can enjoy True Source's Love and Light radiating to our siblings so that we can be instruments rather than getting pulled into dysfunctional relationship dynamics in the privacy of our minds.

Because of the need for healthy boundaries in human relationships, it may be uncomfortable to consider letting go our boundaries with True Source. Some people fear, "If I let go of all my boundaries, I will lose myself." I understand this feeling because I used to experience it myself. *However, to grow spiritually, we have to be willing to let go of our personal ego boundaries that separate us from The Love of True Source. It is a matter of our trust in The Love winning over our fear and the ego's right to remain in separation. The truth is that we do not and will not lose ourselves. Instead of losing ourselves, we become connected to who we truly are. The only thing we can possibly lose is who we are not. What we lose is only the limited games and patterns of our ego, and all the ways our ego has deceived us into thinking that the use of our free will to stay separated from The Love is something beneficial. We lose our armor that has kept us isolated from True Source, living as an independent agent wandering through the universe following our ego's agenda, which keeps on creating additional karmic blockages. Some of us may think we are protecting ourselves when we put on our emotional armor; however, we are actually imprisoning ourselves.*

In any ordinary human relationship, it is important to have healthy boundaries. *There is only one relationship in which it is safe to completely let go of our boundaries, and that is our relationship with True Source. When we let The Love open our heart, dissolving our non-physical boundaries and edges, The Love is then free to remove all our blockages. To the degree that we trust, feel and accept True Source's Love with gratitude, the boundaries of our personal limitations dissolve. Our hearts open so that we can receive all the benefits of being cleansed by The Love, while also having the blessed opportunity to be an instrument of True Source's Love and Light for all beings everywhere.*

Chapter 26
Breaking the Cycle of Work,
Chores and Reward

The depth of our conditioning runs deep. Yet it can be very difficult to recognize this at times because what we consider to be normal is part of that conditioning process. For example, based on how we have been taught from a young age, we may believe it is normal that life is divided into categories of work and reward. We also have a tendency to divide life into the categories of pleasure and pain. Pain becomes a product of what we don't like to do or sensations that are unpleasant. When something is an inconvenience, or if we don't feel like doing something, we may say, "What a pain."

Our ego has perfected the ability to categorize things into likes and dislikes. We view rewards as our 'likes' and view our 'dislikes' as what we have to do in order to get the rewards. That is how things come to be considered chores. For example, "I don't like the chore of having to wash my dishes but I do it because I don't want to get sick eating off dirty plates and I can't stand a dirty kitchen." Not getting sick from dirty plates is our dislike and a clean kitchen becomes the reward.

When we learn to be grateful in every moment, the distinction of chores, work and rewards dissolves. The moments you spend washing dishes are as beautiful as those moments viewing a magnificent sunset. The reason we feel this is because our heart embodies contentment. Our heart is content, just in itself, because our hearts are connected to True Source's Love and Light. When grounded in our hearts, wonderful moments are not defined by what is going on in the external world. Moments are wonderful because of our heartfelt gratitude and connection to the complete Love True Source has for every being. This is why feeling our heart is the path to freedom. By following the heart, our happiness is no longer enslaved, or dependent on what is happening around us. We are happy whether or not we get our likes met or are able to avoid our dislikes.

What many of us do is get hooked on feeling good when external circumstances are going the way we would like them to go. If we need to do something we do not like doing, then it remains a chore. When we get to do something we like, we experience the reaping of a reward. The cycle of work, chores and rewards becomes a merry-go-round. The problem is that a significant portion of time ends up being spent doing all the things we have to do to before we get to the rewards. And for some people the rewards are very short lived, and it can seem like the majority of life is a chore. This is why for some of us, life is basically a 'pain' with very little pleasure.

Our heart is the key for us to stop making the distinction between work and rewards. When our ego is in charge, we are trapped into performing tasks and chores not for the enjoyment of the process but for the expected rewards that may follow.

Being heartfully engaged in gratitude to True Source, no matter what we are doing, is the best reward we could ever reap. Being grateful to True Source in each moment, even for all the small things that happen, is so wonderful. Life becomes much more entertaining when we stop separating work from rewards.

Rewards provide only temporary pleasure, and if we don't realize this, we end up placing such a high value on getting reward after reward; we struggle endlessly and much of our life may seem like a burden. Often, if we indulge in what we consider to be a pleasure for a long period of time, it will lose its attraction. Check with your own life and you will probably see this is true. Even things that were once filled with pleasure become boring after awhile.

When we are grounded in our hearts with abundant gratitude, we realize that the beautiful feelings we are having in each moment are directly based on the experience of our heart, and are not based on external circumstances. When our joy is not based on external circumstances, we can break the chain that keeps us in the bondage of our work, chore and reward cycle. Our heart allows us to let go of the distinction of work and reward, and pleasure and pain. Everything that we do becomes enjoyable, even doing things that our ego previously despised. Washing dishes becomes a totally different experience! So the question in any moment is not, "What do I have to do?" It is, "What is the quality of my heart and my heart's connection to True Source's Love?" Are we ready to stop living for the purpose of just reaping rewards in life? *When we are grounded in our hearts, feeling, enjoying and accepting True Source's Love while being grateful, every moment becomes the greatest reward of all.*

There can be no greater reward than The Love because True Source's Perfect Love is always giving us the best of the best, dissolving our blockages, and removing everything that is not of The Love. When our heart realizes what this means, our gratitude soars, exponentially enhanced. Only True Source's Love can open our hearts and allow us to fulfill the ultimate purpose of our existence. The core of our heart, our inner heart, the spark of Love and Light, realizes exactly what this means because it longs to return to our true Home.

Chapter 27
The Joy of Waiting in Line

In our daily lives, there are always times we have to wait, whether that is in a traffic jam, at the bank, in a restaurant or at the grocery store. Do you enjoy the experience of waiting 10 minutes in line at the grocery store? Typically what some of us do at this time is tap our foot, possibly become judgmental of the employees, while feeling impatient or frustrated that it is taking so long. Or we may drift off into a mental preoccupation with our 'to do list,' our unresolved issues, or unsettled emotions that got triggered from a previous circumstance.

This is a typical response and what we have come to call normal and just one example of what we do in so many different ways throughout the day. *If we are honest with ourselves, we realize that a significant portion of our waking hours is spent enga=ging fragmented thoughts, living in our head, as we wander from past to future preoccupations or from one unsettled issue that triggers the next unsettled feeling.*

In order to grow spiritually, we have to bring the experience of our hearts into our moment-to-moment lives. The understanding of our head might say, "So what is the big deal if I am impatient or frustrated while being on the grocery line? It's my right. Everybody does it and it is normal." This is not just an issue about our right to be so-called 'normal' or that we are not taking the time to smell the roses. This is a very important issue and the core of our heart knows that this is not a small matter. *It is a huge matter, because all of these moments spent in the grocery line or elsewhere, when we are feeling impatient or unsettled, are precious moments, and we are choosing our preoccupation with our ego's agenda over True Source's Love. Essentially, we are turning our back on The Love. Without this realization, it becomes so much easier for us to stay disconnected from True Source's Love because we feel justified in fulfilling our ego's agenda, an agenda to keep us separate from The*

Love.

If a friend or loved one is attempting to communicate something that feels crucial for them to share, then it is important that we be present and empathetic. If they were sharing something with us that they considered to be an utmost priority, and we kept reading the newspaper while shaking our head as if we were listening, it would be very rude behavior. Similarly, it has to become crystal clear to us that this is what we are doing in our relationship with True Source. In each and every moment, True Source's Love wants to communicate with our hearts, because the nature of The Love is to Love us. If we are busy with our ways, habits, and concepts, we are ignoring The Love. We may be spending the majority of our time responding to True Source's Love as if we are busy reading the newspaper. *Preoccupation, emotional reactions and giving importance to trivial things are all part of our ego's agenda to keep us busy, all the while the ego enforces its right to remain separate from The Love.* From my perspective, it is important that we realize it is rude to ignore The Love, because by not accepting The Love, we are turning our back on The Love.

True Source will never force us, because forcing is not the nature of Love. True Love is never compelling, always inviting. True Source is always and continuously inviting us to choose The Love over our right to remain a separate 'me.' We have to realize the consequence of choosing 'me', and the suffering that it brings us, and become disillusioned with our separation. We may think that being separate, or being independent is the path to freedom, when in actuality, the agenda of our ego keeps us indebted to an ongoing prison sentence.

It is time for us to wake up from the illusion of what we have thought freedom to be. Knowingly, or unknowingly, we have conditioned a part of us to think that freedom is our right to live independently, to do what we want, to have what we want and to manifest our dreams.

This definition of freedom fulfills the delights of the soul but does not allow the true nature and freedom of our spirit to grow. Spiritual freedom is related to our non-physical heart being free from all blockages, in all its layers and in all its directions. It is the freedom of no longer being triggered, having no issues with anyone, anywhere, including from anything that ever happened at any time in our soul's journey. Then our heart is completely free to be an instrument of True Source's Love and Light. This is the freedom that our heart longs for which only The Love can give. Thinking that we can obtain freedom by other means is an illusion that we have been carrying through time.

Now is the time to end this perpetual illusion and break free of the ego's concept of freedom. Seeking to fulfill this concept has kept us in bondage and in separation, separate from the complete Love that True Source has for you, me, and everyone. The core of our heart knows that only The Love can set us free.

This is the essence of the bigger picture. It is so much more than the fact that we are stressed or preoccupied in the grocery store line. The freedom to think, to allow an endless stream of fragmented thoughts to distract us, easily becomes our reality when we are not grounded in our hearts. When our ego is in charge, our heart and true self are in a state of disconnect. *Every moment we turn away, disconnected from True Source's Love, we also deny True Source the opportunity to use us as an instrument of The Love and Light.* Every moment we choose to feel True Source's Love, we turn that moment we are waiting on the grocery line into an experience that our hearts can enjoy and be grateful. All the while, smiling to the hearts around us, we are open to feeling True Source's Love radiating to the hearts of all beings around us. In the simple acts of everyday life, we get to participate in the great plan, allowing The Love to do just what The Love wants to do, and that is, to radiate gently, sweetly and freely. Boredom does not need to ever exist. Waiting in line can be a spiritual joy. Our heart can be free to enjoy the beauty and radiance of True Source's Love in each and every moment.

For example, while waiting for my car to be repaired one day, I found myself sitting outside the waiting room choosing to enjoy the experience of True Source's Love. My heart felt so inspired, I decided to dictate this chapter on my portable recorder.

Chapter 28
Our Blockages Run Deep

W e are all in the need of healing because our soul is fragmented and our spirit is not whole. Some people believe that our spirit or true self is already whole, complete and not in need of healing. However, our true self has taken on a soul and physical form so we can exist on the Earth dimension for the purpose of learning and healing. Our inner heart is the very core of our being and it is the only part of us that is pure. The reason for this, is that our inner heart is the spark of Love and Light created by True Source. But our true self has not completed all of its lessons. Our Earth experience is a gift designed for the learning and healing of our spirit so that our true self can become a part of The Love, rather than existing in a state of separation.

If we were not in need of healing, we would feel, trust and accept True Source's Love completely. Our hearts would be relying on True Source's Love above all things in every moment. Our soul, ego and 'I' would be in alignment with allowing our whole heart and whole being to no longer be separate from The Love.

Some new age philosophy claims, "I am God and we are all God." We may mean no harm when we think this, however this can become an illusion the soul can play in order to fulfill a hidden desire to experience itself as a deity. *True Source will always be our Creator, the Highest, the One above All, and our One and Only Parent. As a spirit, our true selves are the sparks or children of True Source. When we go Home, back to True Source, we never dissolve and become the same as True Source. We are not and never will be or become True Source. I feel it is important for us to understand this clearly and never aspire to be the same as the Parent of Creation. This idea is a very, very, dangerous dead-end road. It can unconsciously keep the soul striving to achieve a deity status or to become a lord of a realm.*

Some people will say, "I don't need any more healing because I am already saved." Belief alone cannot save us because belief is a mental construct and not a direct experience through our heart.

Above all things, it is always the quality of our heart that matters. The condition of our heart on Earth reflects the degree of wholeness of our spirit, our true self. *As our true self grows in True Source's Love, we get closer toward the fulfillment of our true nature. Only True Source's Love and Light can grow our spirit; to depend on ourselves or anyone else and think otherwise, is a very dangerous delusion. This is why the direct connection of our heart to True Source is crucial for spiritual growth. As we let The Love open our hearts, only then can The Love grow our spirit.*

Our non-physical spiritual heart contains many layers, metaphorically like rings of a tree. These layers consist of multiple energetic blockages located in the front, back, left, right, upper and lower sides of our heart. Our multi-layered spiritual heart holds the entire spectrum of our unresolved issues, unresolved emotions, un-forgiveness toward others and ourselves, unresolved issues with God, guilt, shame, unworthiness, anger, and many other blockages. *The conglomeration of all of these blockages in the different parts of our non-physical heart tells the story of our past. It is all linked to the collective karma of our soul's journey.*

Psychotherapeutic approaches can assist us in having a more adjusted life. For example they support us in having a healthier ego, healthier relationship boundaries, positive communication skills, decreased trauma or pain from our families of origin, letting go of fears or phobias, enhanced self-esteem, and healing from painful relationships or circumstances in this life. But it is important for us to realize the limits of what psychotherapeutic approaches can do and what they cannot do. For example, psychotherapy is not capable of accessing and healing the karmic blockages from our past journey stored in our soul and in the multiple layers of our non-physical spiritual heart. Only The Love can dissolve our karma without karmic consequence. Other beings are not meant to take on our karma. When another being thinks this is their role, they are acting as a deity. Likewise, mindfulness practices or different meditation modalities are also limited, for they are based on us being the 'doer', the one who is in charge of our meditation. These approaches to therapy and meditation are unable to heal the deep blockages in the inner layers of our being.

There are so many layers of resistance and blockages in our

non-physical heart, that there is not enough time to understand them all or process them. These layers run vast and deep. If we feel we are the ones responsible for having to heal our entire karma from our past journey, the immense proportion of this task will produce pressure. It can also feel like an overwhelming burden. All of these blockages keep our heart contracted in different ways. They create the protective armor which keeps the non-physical boundary of our heart closed thereby keeping us separated from The Love. The only thing that is supposed to be in our multidirectional heart is the radiance of True Source's Love.

All of our issues and unresolved blockages are what keep True Source's Love from being able to use our heart as an instrument. And since True Source's Love never wants us separate from The Love, True Source's Love is always waiting to support us in dissolving everything that is not of The Love. Only when we let True Source's Love dissolve everything that is not of The Love can we become the children of True Source as we were designed to be in the original blueprint. There is no one that can do this for us, including ourselves. It is only by accepting and enjoying True Source's Love with gratitude, that we allow The Love to engage in the process of truly setting us free to become who we truly are.

Chapter 29
We Have Nothing to Prove

True Source is always giving us the best of the best, completely Loving us in each and every moment. Why do we feel that we do not deserve True Source's complete Love? What is it that is in us that is making us feel this way? Or consider the opposite feeling. What if we say, "I don't have any parts of me that feel undeserving of True Source's complete Love." Is it possible that our feeling this way might be a reflection of our inflated sense of self-worth, arrogance, self-righteousness, or grandiosity? We underestimate the cleverness of the ego in determining how spiritual we think we are. If every aspect of our being felt deserving, then our whole heart and whole being would completely trust and accept True Source's Love, and everything not of The Love would dissolve.

Very often, the 'I,' in the name of growing spiritually, will try to perfect its self. But growing spiritually is an experience of the heart, and when our heart comes into spiritual alignment, everything else follows.

Perfecting the 'I' does not lead us Home or reveal our true nature. The ego may say, 'I' will pray and meditate more. God, '*I*' will do more and more to serve you. '*I*' will do whatever you want." The 'I' can play this game, in its failed attempt to achieve greater levels of spiritual perfection. The 'I' wants to please God according to what the 'I' believes will make God happy. The 'I' acts like it wants God to judge 'us' in a favorable light. The problem is, what the 'I' thinks is pleasing to True Source is very different than the perspective we get from our heart.

Our heart knows best because True Source's spark of Love and Light is in the core of our hearts. When the 'I' is in charge of how to please God, the viewpoints on how to please God can range dramatically. For example, someone may be a terrorist and kill in the name of God because his 'I' is telling him that it is holy to kill nonbelievers. Some of us may even follow systems of self-punishment to prove their worthiness before God. We will flagellate or whip ourselves on the back. Others perform acts of penance, sacrifice or suffering, all to prove their commitment to God. The ego is saying to God, "I will show you how much I am willing to sacrifice for You and when You see how much I will sacrifice in Your Name, then You will Grace me, granting my wishes for myself and others."

It is common for many of us to feel driven by a desire to serve humanity or take on a cause. It is wonderful that people want to serve, but it is important for our spiritual growth that we understand the subtle patterns of the ego. Some have experienced that, no matter how much they serve or do for others, it is never enough. I found myself feeling this way for many years. There was always the feeling that 'I have to do more' and I did not even know what that 'more' was. "I want to be a good spiritual person in Your eyes, so 'I' will keep doing more and more to please you, God."

The drive to prove we are worthy of The Love is not coming from our heart. We may mean well, but this approach to spiritual growth is very limited. When we do this, there is a part of us still acting like children looking for approval from our parents. Many of us are seeking confirmation of our worthiness from True Source and that drives us in attempts to prove our worthiness through our good deeds.

This is where the confusion comes in. Our ego will never reach the level of fulfillment we seek, because only our heart has a direct connection to True Source's Love and Light. Our head was meant to support, to facilitate carrying out the orders from our spiritual heart.

In the core of our heart, we know that approval from True Source is not needed because The Love is present always and forever. We have never had to earn True Source's Love. Yet, from our past journey, because our soul has accumulated abandonment and rejection issues, we may feel that we have to somehow prove ourselves, showing True Source that we deserve to be Loved. The very core of our heart knows that True Source never abandoned or rejected us. We are the ones who turned away from The Love. If we ever think that True Source abandoned or rejected us, then, that is our projection.

As previously explained, we also have guilt, shame, un-forgiveness, anger, sadness, hurts and many other blockages in the field of our heart. In addition we have resentment and payback lists and our deep blockages are hiding beyond our conscious awareness.

These are patterns in our soul that keep us from completely trusting and accepting True Source's Love.

We strive to prove our worth, because we feel unworthy of True Source's complete Love.

When I reflect back over my journey, I can remember how I had felt responsible for the sum total of my soul's karma. Not only did I feel responsible for the creation of my karmic accumulation, I felt that I had to be a spiritual warrior ready to do whatever I had to do in order to neutralize all the karmic blockages from my past lives. At that time, I did not realize the immense pressure I was carrying with me. 'I' was the one who had to set the record straight. By my good deeds and actions, or so I thought, I would eventually be able to balance out the past. It was only after my heart experienced that True Source's Love was present in every moment, that True Source's complete Love wanted to dissolve everything not of The Love, that I realized the overwhelming burden I carried, thinking I was the one who had to make everything right. I was relying on 'me', and not on The Love.

Remember, True Source's Love is above the Law of Karma, and The Love is always waiting to give us the best of the best. But, this can only happen when we let The Love have its way. This realization and experience of how The Love wants to dissolve, and can dissolve deep blockages, allows my heart to experience gratitude to True Source in ways beyond anything my mind could ever conceive.

Our heart condition and the willingness of our heart to be grateful, while feeling, enjoying and accepting True Source's Love reflects the degree to which we trust The Love. The core of our heart knows our spiritual worth is not performance-based. It is not about what we have done or what we will do.

True Source's Love for us is unconditional. We are all worthy and deserving of True Source's complete Love, each and every moment, because True Source is our One and Only Parent and we are the children of True Source. When a child is naughty, a healthy earthly parent still loves that child just as they do when the child is well behaved. True Source does not discriminate. When the core of our heart realizes that we have been loved completely, even during the darkest moments of our ancient past, we will never be the same again. In every moment, True Source's Love and Light is calling us Home to be who we are, to be as sparks which are no longer separated from The Love.

The question is never, "Are we deserving?" because from the position of True Source's Love, this question does not exist. The real question is, "When will our hearts be ready to allow The Love to give us the best of the best?" The core of our heart longs to be Home again, and always realizes we are deserving of True Source's complete Love, because the core of our heart realizes that The Love *is* True Source's Will.

We have nothing to prove and nothing to do to demonstrate our worthiness. It is time for our hearts to wake up and simply enjoy, trust, feel and accept True Source's Love with deep heart-felt gratitude. It is so simple; yet we have made it so complex. True Source's unlimited Love is always waiting for every heart to receive and respond to this eternal call.

Chapter 30
It is Time to Choose True Source's Love

As a human race, we do not have a very good track record regarding all the things that have taken place in the name of God. Crusades, wars, and battles over God, have been responsible for millions of deaths throughout every part of the globe. This is an example of what happens when religion is dominated by dogma, ritual and head-centered belief systems. *The dysfunctional behavior of our human family throughout history demonstrates that we have been acting from our heads and not our hearts. If we truly had been in our heart, we would not have engaged in these behaviors, creating ego-based reasons, justifications or excuses to harm others.*

A number of years ago, I was working as a psychologist at a rehabilitation hospital. I had a client who explained to me that if I did not share her particular beliefs, then I was going to hell. I said, "Let me understand your logic. If I believe the way you are suggesting, then I am saved forever, and if I do not believe the way you think I should believe, I am damned to eternal hell forever." With a straight face she said, "Absolutely." This comment came from an educated college graduate. I felt to ask for further clarification. I said, "Let us say that there is a woman from China who lives in a small village in the mountains. She loves God with her whole heart. She has a heart of gold and, even though she is quite poor, she cooks food everyday to feed the beggars and poor people. She has lived her moment-to-moment life with gratitude. This woman has never been exposed to your religion and therefore, she does not share your beliefs. Are you telling me that this woman is going to hell forever because she does not believe the way you think she should believe?" Looking into my eyes with a straight face, she replied, "Yes." What an interesting concept of God she had.

I had another client who said to me I must call God by a certain name. Otherwise, God would not hear me or my prayers and I would not be able to be connected to God. I shared that the name for water in Spanish is *agua* and in Hindi it is *pani*. Whether you say water, agua, or pani, water is water. She expressed, "If you were walking down the street and someone called out John, would you turn around?" I said I would not. She said, "See, if you do not call God by God's real and only name, God will not respond."

These are all examples of how easy it is for human beings to hold tight to concepts and beliefs about religion, spirituality and God. In addition, we may create conscious and unconscious fears about True Source. A lot of spiritual damage can be done from our exposure to dogma in religion. As a result many of us shut down and do not deal with the spiritual aspect of our being because it has been so confusing or presented to us in a ritualistic, bizarre or dogmatic perspective. Having been so turned off by the presentation of religion in ways that were so hypocritical or self-righteous, we may want nothing to do with True Source, our Creator.

We have to let The Love help us heal any and all of these unresolved wounds or doubts so that our spiritual journey can be clear, direct and joyful. By direct, I am referring to a direct heart connection with our Creator. *It is our birthright. We all have the birthright of a direct and intimate connection with our one and only True Parent, the One who created us, as sparks of love, and gave us the gifts of a soul and human body. Then on this earthly dimension, we can enjoy being instruments of True Source's Love and Light, radiating The Love to every being in the whole existence.* This direct intimate heart connection allows our true being to feel True Source's Love, waking us up from our amnesia, allowing us to return Home... to our True Home that we left, a long, long time ago. This is what spiritual growth is really about. When our soul functions as the facility it was designed to be, our spirit, our true self can return Home to our Source.

Regarding death, what matters most is the quality of our heart. How willing is our heart to accept and embrace The Love and Light with gratitude? If we are not able to do this when we have a physical form, why would we assume we are able to do this when we drop our physical form?

So, let me ask a big question. If True Source is the Source of Love and Light, why would True Source ever send our soul to a lower dimension? The answer is that True Source has never sent any soul to a lower dimension and True Source's Love has never abandoned or rejected us.

When a person has their physical body, no matter how heavy they may become with burdens, pressures, guilt, bitterness, anger, shame, resentments, un-forgiveness and unresolved issues, they are typically able to find ways to distract themselves from their suffering and the density of their problems. For example, eating, drinking alcohol, watching TV, engaging in hobbies and sleep are all the ways we use to get a temporary reprieve from the heaviness of our burdens. There are so many ways on this Earth dimension to stay busy and distract ourselves from facing the blockages that lie under the surface.

When a person drops their physical form, there is no place to hide. The different ways that people avoid their burdens and blockages do not exist after they drop their physical form. *We are what we are and death brings us back to our non-physical nature without the protective and insulative covering of our physical form.* The overall experience, the vibration, the nature we had and expressed on Earth is amplified because there is no place to hide. If our heart was attuned to accepting and embracing The Love, then our experience of The Love and Light after death will be beyond anything we experienced in a body while on Earth because the experience is no longer filtered by the density of our physical form.

If someone's heart is closed and heavy, filled with bitterness and burdens, all their emotional pain and anguish will be amplified after death. They will most likely not feel comfortable embracing The Love and Light available because they are still identified with and resonating with the intensity of their burdens and their emotional reactivity.

This is easier to understand if we recall how we are capable of interacting in our intimate relationships after a dispute. If you get into a fight with a loved one and that loved one comes up to hug you, you may push them away saying, "I don't want your hug right now; get away from me." You resist the hug and turn your back on them. Likewise, if a person is vibrating with anger, resentment, fear, shame or unworthiness, they most likely will not feel very comfortable accepting True Source's Love and Light.

True Source's Love is present for every being, unconditionally Loving us and always giving us the best of the best, whether we are in physical or non-physical form. We are the ones who have the option, the choice, to run away, to hide in a dimmer place because we are scared to embrace The Love and Light.

True Source never sends anyone to a lower dimension. Souls go there of their own accord because, filled with shame or resentments, they do not feel comfortable with the brightness of The Love and Light. Imagine a thief in the night, in a parking lot, with sneaky motives, trying to break into a car. When the lights in the parking lot are turned on there is only one thing this thief will want to do: run away from the light and find a place to hide where it is dimmer or dark. They are looking for a shadow in which to hide.

Dimmer dimensions are only temporary resting places. Because True Source has such complete and continuous Love for us, our life journey always presents us with opportunities to choose The Love over our soul's and ego's agendas. *The deepest purpose of our existence is for our true self or spirit to learn to be completely directed to our Creator and to accept, embrace and trust The Love above all things. Our soul and physical form have been given to us as a gift for learning on this physical dimension so that, who we are as a true self can awaken within True Source's Love and Light. Our ultimate destiny is for our true self to return to our Source. Spiritual growth is the journey of our spirit, our true self returning Home.*

True Source does not punish anyone. The idea of a punishing God is a human mental construct. The core of our heart knows that the only quality our Creator has with us is one of pure Love. True Source's complete Love is here in every moment. The opportunity, the pathway, is always present, every moment, for every being to return Home. We can remember again and become who we truly are: sparks of the Creator.

It is important for the core of our heart to realize that never, for one moment, has True Source ever abandoned or rejected us. It is we who fail to embrace and accept True Source's Love. We are the ones who misuse our free will and block True Source's Love from dissolving all of the karmic blockages from our ancient past. We have this life, this opportunity, to learn to use our free will to choose The Love and let True Source bring us out of ego separation, once again to become a part of The Love, never to be separated again.

We do not realize the extent to which the wounds from our past journey influence our capacity to choose True Source's Love, completely accepting The Love in the here and now. For example, if something happened in this life or a past life, and we blame God, saying, "How could you let this happen to me or my family?", then hidden patterns of doubt, fear, un-forgiveness, resentment or even anger toward True Source become stored in the inner layers of our heart. Layers of guilt, shame and unworthiness can also be hiding in the deep shadows within our heart and soul because in our past, we chose to worship power, name or fame over The Love. When we look at history, it is obvious that the past is filled with barbarism. We are all a part of history and we have all had many occasions, both as victim and as perpetrator, when we were far from being in alignment with The Love.

Irritation, frustration and unresolved issues with our earthly parents may also be projected onto True Source and affect our ability to choose True Source's Love. Our heart has to realize that the only True Parent we have ever had is True Source. The relationship to our earthly parents is really a sibling relationship since we are all children of True Source. Even though we play the role, honoring and respecting our earthly parents, our heart must profoundly recognize that our only True Parent is our Creator. When the core of my heart realized this, the joy, commitment and bond I experience with True Source was significantly transformed. My heart knew that True Source is the only parent I have ever had.

Some of us may feel abandoned or rejected by our earthly parents because they did not support us according to our expectations. It is important that we do not project these abandonment and rejection issues onto True Source. The core of our heart knows that True Source has never abandoned or rejected us for even a split second. *When we examine our past history along with all our old patterns of emotional reactions, the misconceptions we had, and our projections, we better understand why we now have so much resistance to letting True Source Love us completely. We need to realize we are the ones who have not yet learned to truly accept True Source's complete Love, and not blame True Source, or fear True Source. True Source's Love is waiting for us to accept The Love, to feel The Love with our whole heart and our whole being. Only then can we let The Love cleanse our heart all the way through, so that all that remains in the field is the radiance of The Love and Light. Then our true self can awaken to its natural and original state and our soul can fulfill its function as a facility, and support the journey of our spirit, our true self, to return Home. Then on Earth, our multidirectional hearts can radiate True Source's Love and Light to everyone, thereby sharing The Love as instruments, in accordance with The Love and the Will of True Source.*

Chapter 31
Trusting True Source's Love

In my journey, instead of choosing True Source and trusting The Love, I came to realize that I was always trusting something else. What I trusted was what I thought was the key to the next step in my spiritual growth. My trust and allegiance kept changing through time. I trusted different meditation strategies, teachers, the power of intention, and my ability to be the observer and witness. Most importantly, I trusted 'me' as the key to spiritual liberation. Although I did learn something from each experience, my spiritual progress was very limited.

It was as if I was carrying a lantern from door to door trusting that I would find something different that would end my search, or someone to light my lantern. What a surprise to realize that the lantern I was carrying for such a long time was already lit by True Source's Love! What I thought was the key to the door never opened the door. I trusted, searched and looked everywhere in vain. It was only when True Source's Love alone opened my spiritual heart that, with sincere remorse, I felt, "Oh Beloved True Source, I looked everywhere for You, looking in all the wrong ways. Instead of trusting You, instead of choosing You, I relied on 'me' and 'my' ways and strategies...all along, failing to rely on You and Your complete unlimited Love that You have for every being. Please bless me to never think again that something else is better than what Your direct Love can give. Beloved, now, I am so grateful...so grateful to You."

When we choose our mind to be the director of our lives, we continue to experience an incompleteness and feeling of separation. Many people feel like their life is an uphill battle, that they are running on a treadmill with no end. Only through our heart can we be complete and bridge the divide of separateness that humans feel. When we choose to be in our mind, the games we are capable of playing with ourselves are quite complex and intriguing. For example, we use excuses and justifications in order to support the belief that it is safer to stay in separation from The Love, and, in fact, many of us believe or feel that opening our heart is risky.

Living with an open heart is the safest way to live. Not doing so boils down to our lack of trust in our own heart, and our mistrust of The Love. Many of us fear that if we really let go and let The Love of True Source embrace us completely, then something bad will happen. What if we lose our selves in The Love, or lose our very existence, or get out of control? In actuality, when we allow the Love to embrace us completely, what gets lost is who we are not. The Love only dissolves all of the aspects we created which have kept us in separation from The Love.

The real you, you as a true self, can never be dissolved and will always be you. Only our self-created ego identity; the 'not you' can be dissolved by The Love. Why hold onto something that keeps us in separation, that is the very root of our pain, and that is not who we truly are? When our heart realizes what it means that True Source's Love is waiting every moment to give us the best of the best, our life's journey will become transformed.

When our heart realizes and begins to accept that True Source just wants to Love us completely in every moment, then our using other methods or techniques, like mantras, mindfulness, intention or anything that is not the direct connection with The Love seems absurd. It's like being so thirsty and furiously digging a well looking for water while someone is present, right there with you, offering to quench your thirst with a sweet glass of water from an eternal well that never goes dry. And you say, "leave me alone, I am busy... Can't you see I am busy digging?"

The deeper meaning of this story is not just about whether or not we choose to accept True Source's Love; it's about what it means when we turn away from the Source of Love and Light. If a parent wants to give their child a hug, and the child turns their back and says "leave me alone, I am busy playing with my toy," well, this is not very respectful. When our heart truly understands this, it feels very arrogant and rude for us to turn away from The Love. This is what we are doing when we hold on for dear life to the right of doing things 'our way,' no matter how justified it may seem. We may choose to hold onto our right to keep digging a big hole, but in the end, all we are left with is a bigger and bigger hole. We fail to quench our spiritual thirst that longs from the core of our heart, to become a part of The Love. Choosing to be the doer, doing everything 'our' way, we will have dug many big holes but we will never be truly whole.

I feel that, if we are truly interested in our spiritual growth, it is important for us to realize that for such a very long time, we have been turning away. We have turned our back on True Source's Love, and instead we have chosen the agenda of our own importance, ways, habits, and concepts. If we protect our agenda and even defend it at all costs, this choice can follow us to the grave and this life will have effectively been for naught. *Yet we tend to protect and defend our right to our agenda because the ego tricked us into believing that doing this is in our best interest. Choosing to follow the ego sent us on a wild voyage through time, a journey that resulted in our gathering a karmic collection of blockages. These blockages burden our hearts, resulting in living a life in which we are not free to fully enjoy, trust and accept True Source's Love.*

In order to grow spiritually, we need to redefine our concept of freedom. Instead of defining freedom as being free to play how 'we' want to play, playing as an independent agent cruising through life, we understand that true freedom is found in the ultimate joy of not resisting the full expression of True Source's Love. We become more and more truly free as we enjoy, trust and accept True Source's Love with gratitude on deeper and deeper levels.

Our head keeps us thinking that we are here on Earth to play out our agenda. *It is important to realize that when we follow the dictates of our ego, we allow our ego to misuse our free will and sabotage our spiritual progress. We exist on Earth to learn to trust and accept True Source's Love, so all that is not of The Love can be dissolved.*

When we hold onto patterns or blockages in our being that are not of The Love, it is like holding onto a painful splinter lodged under the skin. Not only does it hurt, it can become infected. Although you may have been trying for a very long time to get rid of your splinters, you may realize that things are not moving as fast as you would like. When 'we' act as the 'doer,' we only get to scratch the surface while our splinters hide in the shadows of our hearts and souls.

As we begin to truly trust, enjoy and accept True Source's Love, The Love gently dissolves our long-standing dysfunctional patterns and we change rapidly and at times even instantly. When we let True Source's Love give us the best by removing all our blockages and anything we are holding onto that is not of The Love, our purpose then comes into alignment with True Source's Purpose. The core of our heart knows this as truth and is waiting for our whole heart and whole being to join the bigger plan.

Chapter 32
The Joy of Surrender

Who we think we are is a limited version of an incredibly larger truth. Yet we allow this limited version, this copy of who we think we are, to define our concept of what reality is, as well as define how we choose to interact with others and how we will interpret the circumstances in our lives as they unfold. *We act as if the car we are driving is stuck in the mud and we think if we keep stepping on the gas it will get us out of the hole.* When my heart realized how deep the karmic rut that we collectively all share was, and that all our old ways and approaches have failed to get us out from the hole, it seemed ridiculous to continue on the path of 'me' being in charge of achieving spiritual progress. The rut, that is related to the karmic collection that our soul has been carrying through time, is deeper than most realize. We may only be in touch with what we are dealing with in this life.

I kept saying, "I will try harder and harder. My effort, discipline and perseverance will serve me, clear away my karma, and set me free to enjoy my life." This style may help us graduate college, but this approach will not bring us to experience a true spiritual graduation party. I was shocked when I realized that all my effort and disciplined hard work was so limited in regard to my spiritual journey and how far I had actually evolved in spite of all that hard work. This was not an easy realization for me to face, especially after having engaged in thousands of hours in meditation from different traditions. I meditated as the 'doer' in charge of the process. It was as if I was at point A and it was up to me to do 'something' to get to point B. Point B represented spiritual achievement. The *something* I had to do was any meditation technique or style of prayer I was using at that time. 'I' was responsible for the result and it was up to 'me' to demonstrate my commitment, discipline and perseverance.

Many spiritual seekers pursue what is known as 'The Path of

Perfection.' This means it is up to them to be the spiritual warrior who perseveres and reaches the top of the mountain. This is supposed to be done by commitment and refusal to not stop climbing until they reach the top. I followed that approach for many years, and, now, I am so grateful that I no longer carry the heavy burden of feeling personally responsible for having to achieve that level of spiritual perfection.

The irony is that however good we get, even if 'we' become the best of the best, we will still have to surrender because our 'I' is still in the middle of our accomplishment. The ego or 'I' may tell us, "Of course I will help you to surrender", but, it is a joke to think that the ego is interested in surrendering itself.

When we let True Source's direct Love bring us into spiritual alignment, surrendering ceases to be an issue. When we are properly in our hearts, then surrendering, letting go of being in charge, of being in control, becomes joyfully built into the process of embracing and accepting The Love. As we let True Source's Love open our hearts bigger and bigger, unresolved issues and blockages continue to be dissolved. They have to be removed in the process or else the heart would not be able to keep expanding into the gentleness of The Love. Through this process, our true self eventually awakens. Then the consciousness of our soul, ego and 'I' come to happily understand their role in the bigger plan. Our soul and 'I' accept that their role is not to be independent agents exerting their will to maintain separation. The consciousness of the soul becomes loyal to its true purpose, which is to serve True Source and our true self.

This is the path to become who we truly are. *In essence, we were created to be children of True Source, happy to be loved, and to love, sharing the gentleness of The Love impartially to the hearts of all beings, everywhere, in the whole of existence. Surrendering in this way is gentle and joyous, since we are simply letting True Source's Love do everything for us.*

If we think we are going to be able to surrender our ego by our doing through our efforts, or by our reaching for a state of spiritual perfection, then perhaps we are just fooling ourselves. No matter how perfect we become, we will still have to eventually surrender that level of perfection because the spiritual journey is not about how perfect we can become. It is not about how humble we can be or what great acts of kindness and service we can perform. Neither is it about how well we can fast, pray or meditate through the night. In fact, in truth, it is not even about 'us'. It is all about True Source's complete Love for every being.

The biggest sigh of relief I ever experienced happened when I realized it is not about how good I can become, or about how perfect I can be. Neither does our spiritual journey have anything to do with 'me' trying to surrender 'me.' *Ultimately, it is only about True Source's complete Love, Love for you, for me and for every being.* The reason I was so relieved, was that I no longer felt the pressure of being solely responsible for reaching such an exalted saintly state of spiritual perfection. What a relief it was to realize I did not have to find a way to work off or clean up all of the blockages accumulated from this life, my past lives, and my whole epic journey.

When we are willing to let The Love open our hearts, we begin the journey of feeling, trusting, enjoying and accepting True Source's Love in a deeper and more continuous way. Then, The Love and Light of True Source takes care of everything. Yes, everything! True Source's Love is always available, always giving us the best of the best, waiting to bring us Home to where we belong; Home, where once again, we are no longer separated from our Source. This is only possible when we allow True Source to take care of everything. *On our own, we would not possibly be able to take care of everything, since we do not even have a clue as to what 'everything' is.*

Some may say, "Well, since I have so much karma accumulated from so many past lives, it is going to take many lives to work it all off." This understanding is based on thinking that they are the 'doer' in charge of working off all of their karma. The bottom line is that True Source's Love is beyond the Law of Karma, and, if we allow The Love to do it, all our accumulated karma can be gently and quickly cleansed.

This lifetime is a precious opportunity, gifted to us so that we can learn to prioritize and rely on True Source's Love above everything else. By relying on The Love, our true self can return Home while we are in a physical body and, continue on as a part of True Source's Love after we leave this earthly form. This is our journey and where we all belong. We will fail to experience the wholeness that our true self/spirit seeks unless we allow The Love to complete us.

Spiritual surrender is not meant to be a great challenge or something you have to achieve by your effort. It is simply a joy based on your relationship with The Love and Light of True Source. To hug a good friend that you have not seen for a long time is not anything that takes effort or that you have to prepare for. It is easy and natural. This is how easy spiritual surrender is meant to be. But, it will not happen as long as we keep thinking we are the ones who hold the key. Thinking this way means we trust our illusionary key more than we trust The Love of True Source, which is right here and now. Are we ready to realize that we do not hold the key to opening our spiritual heart? *Only The Love is and only The Love will always be the key to bring us Home, back to being our true self. Why? Because we originated from True Source's Love.*

Yet we need to be careful, because believing we are surrendering by letting The Love be the key and the actual experience of true surrender are two very different things. *Just because we think we are surrendering more and more, does not mean that we actually are.* It is hard for us to understand the box that we are living within because we are contained in that box and confined by its walls. If we truly seek spiritual growth, it is time for us to let down our guard, our resistance and the ways in which we protect the walls of our personal box. However, this is easier said than done because the part of us that may be thinking or believing that, "I am surrendering now" is contributing to the illusion that our 'I' is capable of or is actually interested in surrendering itself.

One reason that this spiritual journey is tricky is because we do not fully realize the extent to which we guard and resist the process of letting The Love give us the best. We may say the right words to ourselves such as, "I am ready to let The Love give me the best," and then, off we go, proceeding to be in charge of the process, as we attempt to supervise The Love. Knowingly or unknowingly, due to our lack of complete trust in The Love, there is a part of us that remains as a witness and observer of our experience, and this is the part of us that feels compelled to supervise the Love.

If we totally trusted The Love, there would be no need to remain as a witness because we would realize that when we function as the observer, we are living in separation from The Love of True Source. Yet we may think that being mindful of the 'witness' and 'observer' of our being is an expression of spiritual growth. The reason we feel this way is because being the 'witness' can help us be detached and give us the feeling that we have risen above it all. In addition, when we experience the extended space between our thoughts, along with the resulting temporary lack of emotional reactivity that accompanies this spaciousness, it can also give us the impression that 'I' am being really spiritual in this moment.

In actuality, our being the mindful witnessing observer is a hindrance because we think that the observer is who we are. It is still just 'us' functioning as an independent entity separated from The Love. This mental observer is linked to our soul. It is important to remember, we do not exist to grow the stature of our soul. Our soul exists to serve as a facility for our true self, allowing us to learn from our past mistakes, so we can realize the importance of choosing The Love as our main priority. Spiritual growth then occurs as we let The Love open our hearts on Earth and our true self, our spirit becomes brighter, as The Love dissolves our limiting patterns and negativities. Our true self is naturally brought closer and closer Home.

This is why it is so important to let go of all our previous game plans of how to surrender, and realize 'we just don't know how,' and only The Love can do it for us. Without this humble awareness as the starting point, our attempts at surrendering will be like attempting to run up a straight vertical hill. We may run up the hill, but then, we find ourselves sliding back down.

In the past I can remember thinking that I was surrendering more and more, when in actuality, I was just engaging in the mental process of handing things over with my mind. 'I' thought 'I' was handing over my whole life. The problem is that what I thought of as 'my whole life' was so limited, and just a microcosmic fraction of the very long journey I have been on since separating from True Source. Metaphorically, it is like a big mosaic has shattered. We then pick up one small piece and believe that the 'whole' of who we are is being represented by that fraction. Though we are holding only a very small piece of the mosaic, we act like we know the whole picture. *Our concept of 'I' in this life is only a minute fraction of our long karmic journey and just the most recent page of the book from the biography of our lengthy adventure.*

True surrender involves the surrendering of our whole heart and whole being, including our whole journey since we separated from True Source. We cannot begin to know what that all is, especially from the perspective of the one piece we are holding called our 'I.' And that is why it is so important to surrender our false knowledge of thinking we know, so that we can begin the process of "letting The Love accept us and help us." We have to realize that The Love has been waiting for us for a very long time, and we have been resisting the process because of our attempt to be the one in charge of surrendering.

In the past, my attempts to surrender had a quality of 'reaching' or 'stretching' for the Divine. I can clearly remember meditating in the Himalayas over thirty five years ago and feeling that my journey, my desire for the Yoga of spiritual union was drawing to a close because I yearned for truth so deeply. My yearning was growing stronger, increasing, as a sign that I was surrendering at deeper and deeper levels. 'I' thought 'my' one-pointed commitment to hand over my life meant 'I' was surrendering more and more.

Now, I have come to understand that, when in the past I had those experiences, my 'I,' which was 'reaching' out to surrender, was tainted with my desire to be liberated from the pain of separation. I no longer wanted to suffer from the dictates of my ego. My yearning, my desire, was tainted with these ulterior motives. This type of tainted desire is very different than the pure longing from the core of our heart, the pure longing to reunite with our Creator who is the Source of our spark and true self, and who just wants to Love every being on every dimension completely. However, this pure longing from the core of our heart is only able to awaken to the extent that on deeper and deeper levels, we let The Love embrace us, and we let 'The Love have its way with us.'

What we fail to realize, is that when it is 'us' reaching out to True Source with our desire to surrender, it is our very reaching, our wanting, our hopes and expectations creating a barrier, blocking us from the deeper experience of true spiritual surrender. The true surrender that our whole heart seeks does not happen by our efforts, our commitments, or by our determination to surrender more and more. Even the word 'surrender' implies or conjures up the idea of having to sacrifice or give something up....and that is not what true spiritual surrender is about.

When our whole heart and whole being are expressing our deepest gratitude to True Source, accepting The Love of True Source, then we are on the path of ultimate joy, and we live, and have pure gratitude, for the opportunity to let True Source do what True Source wants to do more than anything. We realize that all The Love wants is to Love all of us completely, so that all of our karmic accumulations can be dissolved, and True Source can bring us Home to where we belong...once again to be a part of The Love and to never be separated again from True Source. When our spiritual heart learns what it means to prioritize and rely on The Love, then the joy of surrendering to The Love just happens effortlessly, in our waking moments and even while we are sleeping.

This book is simply meant to remind us of what we already know in the core of our heart. Reading all of the available spiritual books or even meditating for countless hours as the 'doer' in charge will not support the journey of our spirit returning to our Source. *Only prioritizing and choosing True Source's Love above all things will bring our true self closer and closer Home...and this is what spiritual growth truly is all about. It is simply the journey of our spirit returning to our Source.* Now is the time for us to trust, accept, feel, enjoy and let True Source's Love dissolve all of our blockages so we can be instruments of The Love. Now is the time to allow the gentleness of True Source's Love to be shared with all beings. We are all siblings and are all destined to return to our Beloved True Source. Only then are we walking on the path of true joyful spiritual surrender, and in alignment with our greater purpose.

Chapter 33
The Process of Spiritual Evolution

W e are all part of an evolutionary spiritual process. If I ask, "How would you like to participate in the process of your 'ego's evolution', you may feel your non-physical heart cringe because our heart clearly realizes we are not here for the evolution of the ego. The core of our heart knows we are here on Earth for the purpose of spiritual evolution.

The path of spiritual evolution is the path of our spirit growing from a dim spark to become a part of The Love, living in union with True Source's Will, so that who we are as a being is no longer separate from the Source of Love. This is about our return to our original state and our true nature, the eternally joyful state we once existed in long, long ago, before we separated from True Source due to our desire to be somebody.

Technology is evolving before our eyes and many consider the evolution of technology as being the end goal of civilization. However, I feel that the true progress of civilization is connected to our collective spiritual evolution. Either modern technology can be a great gift, which supports our spiritual growth or it becomes an obsession that consumes us, providing a variety of distractions that keep us disconnected from the real purpose of life. We may become so preoccupied with our busy-ness, that we get stuck in our heads and end up having a superficial existence giving importance to things that do not support us in fulfilling the true purpose of our lives. Technological growth can be wonderful if it is used as a vehicle to support our spiritual growth.

In order for us to evolve spiritually, it is important for us to have a clear understanding of what spiritual evolution means. As shared before, it means the development of our spirit and not the cultivation of our soul. *A soul that becomes stronger and able to exert power to manifest, influence energy or circumstances, or can impress others with its radiant grandiosity, should not be confused with spiritual evolution.*

In this chapter, I will be sharing about some meditation approaches I had practiced in the past. If anyone is practicing these modalities, I apologize if any of my comments are found offensive to you. I felt it was important for me to share about some of the limitations I personally experienced. And yet whatever I practiced in the past provided such wonderful lessons. Everything I have done through the course of my journey, feels to be beautiful stepping stones to help me learn, and now realize that The Love of True Source can do beyond what 'I' can achieve through any technique.

Beginning in the 1970's, when I was practicing a particular method, I believed that I was growing spiritually, though I now have a different realization about what spiritual evolution really means.

For example, when I practiced meditation through the use of a mantra, and other yoga meditation practices, I felt positive results though now realize that my experience fell more into the category of soul enhancement and stress management. Even though I reached a state where I experienced the space between my thoughts and breaths, my soul was in charge of the process. I did experience physical, mental and emotional benefits. However, our being the 'doer' of whatever practice we choose does not grow our true self, our spirit. Only The Love does.

Real spiritual growth takes place only to the degree that we rely on The Love of True Source to open our spiritual heart. As we let The Love cleanse and open our hearts, our spirit, our true self grows in True Source's Love. The deepening quality of the relationship of our heart to True Source's Love is directly linked to the unfolding of our spiritual evolution. If we want true spiritual evolution, relying on True Source's Love to open our spiritual heart is essential.

Many years ago, I also engaged in spiritual chanting with others often lasting for many hours at a time. We went into what felt like trance states that were very highly charged. As I reflect back on my chanting experience, I realize that the feelings of devotion to God that were generated were more like a very exhilarating emotionally-charged sensation. From the repetition of the chanting I also felt that the restless thoughts in my mind were temporally being suspended. I was reaching out to God, as if it were up to me, as if I had to be the one who reached out high enough with 'my' total devotion, sincerity and 'my' willingness to surrender. Basically, I was the 'doer' responsible for bridging the divide with the Divine. That is why I now feel that my early experience of being devotional was sentimental and emotion-based and did not come from a pure spiritual heart experience.

We cannot experience our hearts by being the 'doer' because only The Love of True Source is able to bring us into our hearts. It is not about how perfect we can become or how high we can reach. Our trying, all our effort, is just the illusion of our mind attempting to get us to believe that our ego is really interested in surrendering itself or that through the door of the ego we can spiritually evolve. However, because our mind is in charge of the process, we may not think we are doing this, though this is in fact what is happening. When the ego is in charge, we trust our ways rather than truly trusting the way of The Love. If spiritual chanting or dance leads to a spiritual experience, it is not a result of our being the 'doer.' It occurred because in our quietness we just let go and allowed True Source's Love to touch our hearts.

When we relax and let go of our ways and let The Love bring us into our hearts, we may not necessarily stop thinking. As we function in the world, we still experience our thoughts, but now our thoughts arise from the inspiration of our heart and are no longer motivated by the agenda of our egos.

In the past I also studied Oriental systems such as *chi kung* (*qi gong*) and Taoist internal cultivation. Throughout these practices I learned to use my attention, my mind, to feel the "life force" (chi), training my mind to circulate chi through different energy channels. I used different ways to move chi energy with my intention. I experienced some health benefits and a deep sense of balance, harmony, flow and rhythm. However, I also strengthened 'my' will and soul, while cultivating the power of the soul's ability to use intention. In the name of co-creating with the universe, my sense of personal power grew and became amplified. Regarding spiritual evolution, I have come to realize that true spiritual growth is not about the development of our soul or personal power.

Many people are committed to their mindfulness practice. I previously taught mindfulness training, biofeedback and other meditation modalities in a variety of community settings such as rehabilitation hospitals, universities and prisons. There are positive therapeutic benefits which students, inmates and clients received. For example, clients in deep despair suffering from chronic pain conditions received wonderful benefits.

From the perspective of spiritual growth, I feel mindfulness practice can be a potential trap that leads to a plateau that can be difficult to navigate beyond. I understand that this may be a controversial statement because many people practice mindfulness meditation as an important part of their spiritual journey. I share my views because I have seen in my own life how using the mind like this can become a hindrance to our real spiritual journey. Typically, when we are practicing mindfulness, we are perfecting the art of becoming an observer of our thoughts, feelings, and actions. From the level of the mind it can feel quite freeing and even enhance the perception of our senses. Mindfulness allows us to be in a state of awareness where we can observe, "Ah, there I go again kicking myself in the rear end", or "Ah, there I go again becoming judgmental", or "Ah, there I go again worrying about something that may never happen." It is so wonderful when we begin to observe our drama rather than identifying with it, and this is one of the benefits of mindfulness.

From my experience, it can also consume energy to be mindful. It takes energy to monitor our thoughts, to be on the lookout for emotional weeds or non-productive cognitions that begin to surface, and to make sure that weeds do not take over the garden of our mind. Although observing a pattern in ourselves helps us to detach and reduce the intensity and frequency of those patterns, it is rare that the pattern will be completely eliminated. It takes commitment to stay diligent as the overseer so that our limiting patterns and tendencies can be held in check. I found in the past, that not only does this take energy; it can also turn into a battle with competing parts of ourselves. It takes effort, vigor and due diligence to not get pulled into the dramas in our everyday lives. When we learn to allow The Love to bring us into the no-drama zone of our hearts, we naturally and effortlessly enjoy the here and now. When we are deep within our hearts, there is no need to oversee the potential unruly tendencies of the mind. We are in connection with The Love of True Source and everything is part of that calm and peaceful flow. Once we learn to experience heartfulness, we realize the limitations of mindfulness.

As previously explained mindfulness helps us to be aware of our drama rather than being in the middle of the drama. We may even reach a state of detachment whereby we think we have risen above our drama. Our mind becomes still, silenced from all chatter. Thoughts and emotions temporarily cease to exist and our mind experiences a very calm space of awareness. We can easily enter into the space between our thoughts, even the space between our breaths, and experience a state that feels very spiritual, according to our conceptual understanding of what it means to be spiritual.

I now realize that when I achieved this state, it was my soul that experienced this heightened state of awareness and sense of connection. It is like becoming the observer of the process with no process left to observe. I remained as the witness with no thoughts surfacing onto the stage of my mind. *Being mindful, or the observer of our process, however, can significantly interfere with our ability to feel, enjoy, accept and rely on True Source's Love.* I trained myself to be such a good observer that this aspect of my consciousness witnessed my heart the way it observes thoughts or emotions. However, observing my heart kept me disconnected from my heart and blocked my experience of feeling the direct connection to True Source's Love. *Just as being an observer through mindfulness practice allows us to witness our drama, it also can result in our heart becoming a separate object which is experienced from a distance.*

There are advanced states of mindfulness practice where the sense of subject and object dissolve and thoughts effortlessly cease to be. There is no sense of engaging in a 'practice' or in being the 'doer'. From my heart's best understanding, this spiritual state is available because The Love of True Source is able to flourish in the absence of thought, desire, and personal agenda. When we give credit to True Source, rather than giving credit to ourselves for achieving a spiritual state, a natural humbleness and deep level of gratitude is experienced. If we think 'I' achieved this spiritual state, then the soul is in the middle of our perception and in the middle of our sense of accomplishment. Even though we may have had a wonderful spiritual experience, when we take credit, the result is the formation of spiritual arrogance. The expression of this arrogance can be subtle and difficult to recognize.

The true process of spiritual evolution is the journey from our head, our ego, to our heart. As you begin to feel your heart, it is a normal part of the process to simultaneously become aware of how you are mostly observing your heart. As we begin to feel and enjoy our heart, being mindful and dispassionately observing our heart, is like watching a beautiful party that is happening in our heart from a distance. Your non-physical heart may be opening more as you learn to feel The Love and you are beginning to really enjoy the party. Yet there is a big part of you that remains as the observer, out on the balcony peeking through the window. Being an observer, you remain in a state of separation and you do not directly feel the full experience of being touched, and embraced by The Love of True Source.

It is important when we come to realize that the part of us that is observing our heart does not fully trust our heart and it does not completely trust The Love of True Source. That is why it feels safer for it to remain in control at a distance. If that observer completely trusted our heart and The Love of True Source, it would jump into the party so fast, never again to be separated from The Love. True Love never compels or forces us to surrender, but is always gently inviting us to let go. Getting comfortable with letting The Love bring our observer into our heart is a process that is done in stages. It is like going into the water up to your ankles, and when you feel safe with how good it feels, you can go up to your knees.

The main point is that when we rely on our ways to evolve spiritually, we will not get very far, despite our best efforts and good intentions. When we learn to feel and enjoy The Love, we naturally begin to let go and trust The Love, and when we begin to accept and rely on True Source's Love, our spiritual evolution can occur at tremendous speed. If we hit a plateau, it is not because The Love is limiting our spiritual growth. It is because in some way, we are still observing, or controlling, and limiting how much we allow The Love of True Source to give us the best of the best. True Source is incapable of withholding Love, because Loving us completely is the nature of True Source's Love. If ever we feel that we have stagnated, we do not have to look very far to find the culprit. Just look in the mirror. True Source's Love is always with us, guiding and helping us, supporting the completion of our spiritual evolution.

How willing are we to let The Love fulfill its nature, which is to Love us completely, so that everything not of The Love can be dissolved? Letting go of our resistance means that we no longer have to be separated from The Love. This allows our true nature to be experienced and fulfills the ultimate purpose of our existence. The spark, our true essence, within the core of our heart, fulfills its longing to return to our original Home which we left a long, long time ago. *However the spiritual journey is not just about us. It is about all of us. It is about True Source's complete Love for every being. Our true purpose on the Earth dimension is to be an instrument sharing and radiating the gentleness of The Love to support the spiritual evolution of all beings.*

Chapter 34
The Awakening Process

There are many self-created obstacles that, until released, can hinder the awakening process. Among them are our aligning with personal desires, our emotional reactivity, holding on to old habits, and limiting concepts, all which lead us down a very confined path, while we think we are following the path of truth.

When we live from our ego, we have the potential to become extremely self-centered. Whatever ways we think that we might benefit takes precedence over all things. Without realizing it, we utilize our free will to make these poor choices. As a result of greediness, we, along with the environment, can and often do suffer. In addition, when we fail to realize the truth about ourselves, we can be like a child, a two-year-old stuck in the 'temper tantrum' stage who has not yet learned about the importance of sharing. We may become addicted to our sense of power and live in the illusion that having more power will bring us fulfillment. Blinded by our sense of entitlement, we continue to find ways to justify our poor choices.

The beginning of the awakening process occurs when we realize that we exist for something beyond just our self-centered fulfillment. When our minds are in charge, we often use our free will in ways that do not support our highest good. When our ego is at the helm, our thoughts, desires, expectations and emotional reactions drive our behavior.

And even if we do not act out those thoughts, desires and emotions, energetic blockages are still created. We continue to contaminate our non-physical heart during the times we experience arrogance, judgments, resentments or other emotions in the silent false privacy of our minds. Some of us would like to think that if we do not outwardly express the emotion then we are saved from this contamination. This is not so. Blockages are still created from thought. So, it is an illusion to think there is refuge in our ego. As we begin to realize this, we can start to learn to immediately rely on The Love of True Source to remove those blockages. This is one of the great gifts from The Love that is available to us.

Another important stage in our awakening process occurs when we start to sense that we are more than our egos. I remember first experiencing this when I began college and took a philosophy class. I walked into the classroom and written on the chalkboard in big letters was, "WHO ARE YOU?" I thought to myself, "Wow, I am 18 years old and who I think I am is just a product of the programming and conditioning I received from my family, school and neighborhood." I began to realize that I did not have a clue about who I really was beyond the façade I presented to the world. I knew something existed beyond who I had come to think and believe I was. And, like numerous other people have shared, experiencing nature had been a wonderful way to help me realize that there is a grand design, one that exists beyond my human comprehension. In fact, many people first begin to awaken from the trance of their ego through a deep connection with nature.

Connecting to the beauty and mystery of nature helps us to feel a sense of belonging to something that is so much bigger than we thought we were. It is important that we do not plateau at this stage of awakening. We risk getting stuck at this juncture if we believe nature to be the highest expression of spirituality. When we lose ourselves in the magnificence of nature, beautiful heart feelings do become activated. We may even give credit to nature for that majestic experience, instead of giving credit to the Creator.

It is our direct connection to True Source's Love that is at the root of all of the wonderful feelings from the heart such as peace, joy, happiness, gratitude, and love. Nature is awesome. It is the artwork of True Source. However, attempting to align with nature as our spiritual end goal is very limiting. Connecting to the beauty of nature can be very deep and wonderful, yet, as we begin to use our heart properly, we come to understand this connection can only take us so far. Nature may be awesome, but it is limited. For example, it is just a matter of time before our Sun will be extinguished and Earth will cease to exist. True Source's Love is unlimited and created all of existence, including nature. *Nature is a beautiful gift for us to enjoy but not the end-all of what our heart seeks.* Therefore, it is important not to have our praise and our hearts misdirected to nature, or any kind of limited, intermediary experience.

As I have shared throughout the book, our soul and physical

form are gifts from True Source that serve as facilities, so that our hearts can open and our spirit, our true self, can awaken to fulfill its true purpose. And like our soul and our physical form, nature can serve as a wonderful facility to help us realize the wondrous splendor of True Source.

Our head may have a concept about what it means that "True Source loves us unconditionally." Yet to the mind this is a just a concept, not a living experience. The mental constructs that our egos behold can never replace the direct experience of True Source's Love that our spiritual heart can enjoy. There is a profound gratitude in that direct experience that is beyond words.

For our awakening process to unfold, we have to realize that our concepts and mental constructs are limited. We can understand that drinking water can quench our thirst, but this understanding, or even imagining that we are drinking water, will not properly quench our thirst. Just as only drinking the water will alleviate our thirst, only the direct experience of True Source's Love can fulfill the deepest longing that resides in the core of our hearts.

The belief among many spiritual seekers that he or she has already achieved salvation and is free can become a hindrance to freedom, because although they think that they have obtained it, they are merely imagining their freedom. *Even if our belief system tells us we are free, we are only free to the extent that our spiritual heart is open and free, free to allow the gentleness of True Source's Love to radiate in all directions without limit.*

Awakening from the trance of our emotional experience is another vital step in the awakening process, because we may be confusing the sensation of emotion with feeling the experience of True Source's Love. As human beings we often feel very strong sensations while experiencing very high-powered emotions. We may mistakenly think we are having a strong religious or spiritual experience. Often the sensation of emotional passion can become so intense that we assume our spiritual heart is opening and that we are having a pure heart connection with True Source. But all these sensations are not the same as directly experiencing The Love of True Source and are very limiting. Beyond the experience of the most powerful passionate emotions, is that Love of True Source, which is so very gentle. The Love is beyond any limited emotional expression a human being can have.

It is also easy for us to get addicted to strong emotions that are associated with an adrenaline rush, or thrilling emotional sensations.

As a result we may keep trying to recreate them throughout our lives because we confuse this rush of sensation with having a pure spiritual experience. It is also possible to become so entranced with strong sensations that one may yell and scream, fall to the ground or become spellbound.

Having stronger and stronger emotions and sensations will never satisfy us, nor does it mean that our spiritual non-physical heart is opening. Only The Love of True Source fulfills us and opens our heart, not our intense emotional expressions.

As the awakening process continues we begin to become aware of our unique personal soap opera. Previously we could become angry, arrogant, resentful or judgmental and not even realize we were doing that. Now, as we awaken, we become more aware that we are engaging in these or other emotional patterns. We can step back and be the observer of our drama rather than playing out our emotional reactions without awareness. This is one of the benefits of being mindful. It allows us to step back and be a witness. I can remember getting stuck at this stage of my awakening because I thought that if I perfected my ability to be the witness, then I would be able to disconnect from all self-created dramas and possibly achieve spiritual perfection. However, cultivating this observer quality of consciousness caused me to remain in separation from my spiritual heart.

With anything that we do as the 'doer', whether being a witness of our thought processes, or as the one doing a spiritual practice, we are still relying on 'us' as the key to bridge the gap between our state of separation and The Love of True Source. From my experience, this willingness to rely on our selves is the biggest trap of them all and sometimes very subtle and hard to recognize. Even when we think we are not being the 'doer,' if 'we' are practicing, if we are doing a technique, then we are definitely in charge of our awakening, and thinking we are responsible for our transformation.

Someone may say, "But all that is happening is that I am aware of my breath, experiencing the space between my thoughts. What is wrong with that?" Well, in this case, what is wrong is that their 'I' is still 'doing' something. The 'I' is following the flow of breath and the 'I' is aware of space. The same applies regarding the use of mantra. Even if a mantra is used as a bridge to bring us to the space between our thoughts, if the 'I' is doing the chanting, the ego and the mind are still dominant. If we are using our intention to circulate energy or manifest our dreams, we are being the 'doer' in charge.

These are all examples of mindfulness or soul strengthening experiences; however, these are not the same as having the experience of letting The Love of True Source bring our whole heart and whole being into The Love. *The core of our heart contains the spark of True Source's Love and Light and this spark, our true essence, longs for reunion. This process of awakening can only unfold as long as we rely on The Love above all things and exclude using any of our ways, our efforts, concepts, and habits.*

If we are honest with ourselves, we will most likely admit that our mind can be so very tricky, and at times quite misleading. This is why learning to rely on the guidance from the core of heart, because our inner heart is the unblemished pure aspect of our being that has a direct connection to True Source, is so important. One of the biggest obstacles I faced in my spiritual journey was the misconception that as the mindful observer, I could simultaneously experience being deeply connected to my spiritual heart. Many of you reading this book may have this same assumption and believe you are growing spiritually. And even though you may think you have already experienced your spiritual heart, you may have only scratched the surface.

This is what I came to realize even though I thought I was 'advancing'. As the observer, I easily reached states in which I transcended thought and believed I had risen above it all. I believed, 'this is it'. This is an example of how the mind and our concepts can be deceiving. I did not realize that I chose to continue being the observer because I did not completely trust The Love. I feared what would happen if more and more of the observing consciousness were allowed by the Love to be submerged into the depths of my spiritual heart. Since The Love is always the most gentle and will never force us, it is only by allowing The Love to submerge our observer into our hearts, that the spiritual evolutionary process can be exponentially accelerated. If the mindful observer stays fully intact as the witness, you can grow your soul, but the growth of your spirit will be limited. The more you observe, the less of The Love you receive, and it is only The Love of True Source that opens our heart. The quality of our heart mirrors the condition of our spirit, our true self.

If we keep thinking and practicing as though we are responsible, feeling that it is up to us to 'do' something to get from where we are to the place that will result in spiritual completion, then we are being the 'doer.'

When we place any intermediary between our heart and True Source, then we are denying ourselves the opportunity and blessing to have a direct connection with our Creator. The biggest possible shift in our spiritual journey begins when we realize that, for so very long, we have been relying on ourselves or relying on another being as the key to our spiritual progress. At some point with humble and sincere remorse, our heart may feel something like, "Oh, True Source, I am so sorry for my arrogance. I was relying on me, thinking that I can do this better than You, and that my effort is better than what Your Love can do for me." At this point, if we are sincerely humble, we are ready for an authentic, deep awakening and transformation beyond anything we could ever accomplish for ourselves by being in charge. The problem may be that, at this time, we may not be willing to let go of our ego's agenda and our right to do things our own way. We may still be attached to the agenda or radiance of our own soul.

When someone begins to rely on The Love of True Source, as they are feeling, enjoying and accepting Love, True Source's Love begins to open their hearts. There are different stages in the opening of the spiritual heart. For example, one begins to feel beautiful feelings in their heart but, at the same time, they are also aware that their mind is observing their heart. Over time, enjoying the beautiful feeling of the heart becomes easier. As our trust in The Love grows, we are able to relax and enjoy, while observing, and trying much less. The observer does not submerge all at once; it happens in stages according to our trust in The Love to help us.

There is also a stage when, while feeling the beautiful feeling of True Source's Love in our hearts, we begin to realize our feeling is going so beyond anything we have ever experienced on Earth. At another stage, at the same time we are enjoying gentle heart feelings, we may also have emotions and strong sensations that are surfacing. While enjoying feeling The Love radiating through our heart, our experience may be mixed with strong emotional sensations.

What feels like spiritual ecstasy is being fed by the part of us still having emotion. Very often these emotions are part of a cleansing experience and are not new emotions being created. They are surfacing, just to be dissolved by True Source's Love. At yet another stage, emotions can arise as a type of defense mechanism so a boundary can form to comfort us and protect us from our fear of losing our personal space. Of course, no matter what comes up, everything we go through provides a wonderful learning opportunity for us to rely on The Love above our tendency to follow the agenda and ways of our ego.

Heart experiences can be very moving and deep because they

are so different from what the ego considers normal. Tears can flow for an extended period, tears of joy caused from feeling so moved and touched. There can be a feeling of rapture, feeling a divine experience that can last for hours. When we are having this experience, it may seem that this is it, the most profound and enjoyable experience of our lives. The good news is that we are just beginning to receive all of the gifts that True Source's Love wants to give us. It is important for us not to get attached to these feelings and to realize this is only a stage and not the final goal. From a spiritual perspective, becoming attached to any strong feeling can lead to getting addicted to these strong, beautiful sensations. These strong sensations which we may label as 'spiritual' can be so overwhelming and moving that it can feel like we are going to explode with joy. The problem is that the parts of us that are experiencing these strong sensational experiences are separated from the sublime gentleness and sweetness of True Source's Love.

Any part of us that experiences having a strong sensation is a part of us that has not dissolved in the gentleness of True Source's Love. The gentleness of The Love is so very soft. When a mother breastfeeds or is in communion with her new born child, it is not a strong sensational experience. It is a very soft, gentle and sweet communion. Similarly, as True Source's Love opens our spiritual heart more and more, the experience gets softer and gentler; not stronger and stronger. Staying focused on strong sensations will keep us limited, stuck in the experience of those amplified sensations and can create addiction to the 'high'. This prevents us from experiencing deeper and deeper levels of the gentle sweetness of True Source's Love.

To let go of our strong sensations, we have to trust The Love in a more intimate way. Those strong 'wow, wow, wow' sensations create and sustain edges or boundaries to our heart. Our attachments to these sensations keep us from letting the gentleness of True Source's Love move deeper and deeper into the inner layers of our heart. These attachments and boundaries become a way to keep us in separation from True Source's complete Love and limit our ability to become instruments of True Source's Love and Light. Without these limitations, we can enjoy letting the gentleness of The Love radiate through our whole heart, radiating out to the hearts of all beings on all dimensions in the whole of existence.

Only when our whole heart and whole being has dissolved in the gentleness of The Love, can we be instruments according to the

Will of True Source. That is the deepest meaning of "Let Thy Will be Done." This is the opposite of "My will be done."

Simultaneously, while we are enjoying being instruments, The Love begins to dissolve all of the blockages in the inner layers of our heart that keep us separated from The Love. The deeper meaning here is that True Source Loves us so completely, The Love forgives us, continuously, wanting to remove all the karmic blockages of our ancient résumé so we do not have to suffer painfully from the poor choices we have made, from following our ego and from misusing our free will. Our heart has to realize what this means and, once we do, we will never be the same again. We will start to become very happy, gratefully giving up our 'right', the right that our ego has imposed on us, to misuse our free will. When we allow The Love to work, helping us to dissolve the domination of our ego, then we can allow "Thy will be done." Our spiritual awakening is accelerated and our journey becomes more and more joyful. This is the process of relying on True Source's Love and letting The Love bring us back Home to our original nature. Then we can be who we truly are, filled with eternal gratitude, enjoying feeling True Source's complete Love for every being. This is the awakening process, the true spiritual journey of our spirit, our true self, enjoying returning to our Source. The true journey is not the journey of our soul ascending to a higher dimension.

A soul that ascends to a higher dimension is still carrying the remaining storehouse of karma and unresolved blockages from its previous journey through time. But in reality, our soul, instead of aligning with the ego and placing its own development above all else, has the blessed opportunity to serve as a facility for our true self to learn and complete the spiritual evolutionary process. Then we are utilizing our soul for the purpose for which it was given to us by True Source. Our soul has to first realize the role it is meant to play in the bigger plan. Without this deep inner realization, our soul will continue to align with the ego and act as an independent agent thinking its purpose is to climb or achieve a higher realm while still carrying karmic baggage and blockages on its back.

The ultimate lesson is for our whole heart and whole being to continuously choose, accept and rely on The Love of True Source, feeling grateful in every moment and in every circumstance. This allows us to share The Love and Light of True Source to the heart of every being, while all karmic blockages within us and everything that is not of The Love, is being dissolved. Our spirit, our true self, awakens in True Source's Love and is able to fulfill the purpose of our existence. The very core of our heart realizes this truth. The deep inner longing of our spark, our true essence, wants only to become a part of The Love and to return to our original Home.

Chapter 35
Spiritual Normality

When I was a young man one of my favourite college courses was cultural anthropology because it helped me begin questioning what it means to be 'normal'. What is normal? One culture says eat a cow but don't you dare eat a pig. Another culture says eat a pig but don't ever eat a cow. There are so many different views about what is normal. In Western culture, the amount of anxiety, depression, ADHD and antipsychotic medications are alarming, yet these have become a normal trend.

What the largest percentages of people do is traditionally classified as normal. When it comes to spiritual approaches, the largest percentage of us feels it is 'normal' to try, to observe and to look for results. That it is 'normal' to be in charge of the process, to act as the 'doer', and to be the one responsible for getting us from our starting point to a greater point beyond that. It is up to 'us' to make progress through our doing. We do not typically consider it 'normal' to progress at anything by doing nothing. Our ego feels it has to do something in order to progress. For most of us, the notion of just accepting and relying on True Source's Love to give us the 'best of the best', seems way too simple.

We do not want to define our standard of normality to be what the ego consciousness has come to define as so very real. If we experience our ego consciousness as reality, then we will never question whether a deeper being lies within. Society considers 'normal' to be a state of drifting from one mental preoccupation to the next, along with a variety of emotional reactions to events. *We have to redefine our definition of what 'normal' means or else our spiritual growth process will be very limited.*

We do not realize that we may be living in a box with fixed walls. *If we use our past experiences of human love to be our compass for comprehending Divine Love, we will have a very limited understanding.*

We have to allow our past understanding about what love is to evolve, because our experience of love is based on a human model and limited definitions of love. 'True love' is not an emotionally-charged experience. Neither is it the Romeo and Juliet version of feeling swept off our feet. True love, The Love of True Source, is so gentle, beyond gentle, sweeter than sweet, and softer than soft.

When I was in college in the early 1970's, many of us were on a search for an 'altered experience.' People were in rebellion against the dogma inherent in religions. Many of us attempted to seek spiritual answers through experimentation with mind-altering substances such as psychedelic mushrooms. I do not recommend this approach because it is not necessary. Our heart holds the key and is available to us in every moment. Some report that the psychedelic experience helped them realize that there is something beyond the conditioning of the ego. There is a risk of becoming caught by such an experience, and even today, people continue to use mind-altering substances as if they were a means to an end. Any beautiful or moving experience achieved from using psychedelic mushrooms can only ever be a very minute fraction of the profound beauty that can be experienced from the connection of our heart to True Source's complete Love for you, me, and everyone.

What we refer to as an altered or peak experience with nature or a special moment in a relationship is not meant to be a rare or special occurrence. Those experiences are meant to remind us of what it means when we are in alignment with our heart. *The experience of being grounded in our heart, feeling that each moment is a moment of heartfelt gratitude and connection to True Source's Love, is our new definition of 'normal' and the state in which we were designed to live. The ego consciousness that we have called 'normal' is meant to be a temporary experience that reminds us that we have disconnected from our hearts. Once felt, we become inspired to let The Love bring us back to our normal joyful experience of being an instrument of True Source's Love and Light.*

Being stuck in ego consciousness is like having a bone out of place. If someone was born with a bone out of place and always lived with pain, they might adjust to think it is normal. Likewise, much of what we have considered to be normal is like being disjointed. We may adapt and forget how painful it is.

After experiencing being in our heart for an extended period of time, when we allow a circumstance to pull us out of our hearts and back into our old ego patterns, we quickly recognize how painful it really is to be living in our heads.

If someone's house is very untidy and dirty, a wrapper on the floor may go unnoticed because it blends in with the mess. On the other hand, if someone's house is spotless and clean, that wrapper would stand out like a sore thumb.

After we have experienced letting The Love bring us deeper and deeper into the inner layers of our heart, while dissolving our blockages along the way, our old ego-dominated patterns that used to seem so normal to us, may now feel intolerable.

This is what we actually want to have happen. Our heart is then recognizing the pain of being separated from The Love. *After we have grown in our ability to feel, enjoy, trust and accept True Source's Love, then, we notice more readily the moment when we get pulled out of our hearts into ego games, and it becomes much easier for us to let Love bring us back into The Love. We don't resist, try, observe or interfere with the process. Instantly, we are brought back into the gentle enjoyment of The Love and this begins to be our permanent Home rather than a temporary residence. We are awakening, and the gentleness and tenderness of The Love becomes our standard of what it feels like to be 'spiritually normal' The more of us who begin experiencing our heart as normal consciousness, the easier it will become for others to easily flow into a natural state of 'spiritual normality.'* The Love of True Source is always waiting to bring us back to where we belong.

As the spiritual evolutionary process unfolds by our allowing The Love of True Source to remove the blockages from our heart, then we begin to trust The Love in a much deeper way. Trusting True Source's Love is not simply a mental experience. It is about our heart learning to trust, and this is demonstrated by a deep shift in the attitude of our heart. As this process unfolds and our hearts become more free and willing to feel, enjoy and accept True Source's Love, then we become instruments of The Love in our waking hours, as we engage in different tasks throughout the day.

A remarkably effortless direct connection is created with The Love and Light of True Source. It is so beautiful. We become capable of experiencing this connection naturally and with ease even when we are engaging in our daily activities on Earth. Naturally, effortlessly, our gratitude flows toward True Source while simultaneously our hearts are accepting the gentle sweetness of True Source's Love. This is not an idea, concept, or emotional experience. This is a core heart connection and the relationship is very deep, tangible and real.

Some spiritual traditions may have a practice in which they use prayer beads. As they move their fingers from bead to bead, they chant the name of God with focus and intent. The natural effortless spiritual experience I am talking about is very different. We do not have to consciously chant the name of True Source or any name for God. We can let go, resting in the feeling that our heart is in communion with The Love, relaxing in the enjoyable connection with The Love while we talk, walk, drive or do whatever it is that we do. This is not to say that the effortless connection will not be broken. However, the good news is that our willingness to feel the gentleness of The Love will instantly bring us back into heart connection.

When we reach a certain level of trust and let The Love dissolve the blockages in the inner layers of our multidirectional heart, then it becomes natural for our free will to choose The Love over our ego's agenda. It is no longer a struggle because it has become the natural attitude of our spiritual heart to choose The Love. In the past, we were not able to do this properly because of all of the accumulated blockages from our karmic history. In addition, our free will was habituated to being misused by our ego in order to fulfil the ego's agenda. We are not here to fulfil our will; we are here to let The Love and Will of True Source be done through our whole heart and whole being.

It is important for the core of our heart to realize that True Source never wants us separate from The Love. We chose to be separate. True Source's Love has always been waiting, in every moment, even during our darkest moments, to bring us back to where we belong. In order to awaken and remain in the spiritual flow, we have to allow our free will to choose True Source's Love. We have to realize that this is not a burden or a sacrifice. It is pure joy. Our heart has to realize that when our free will chooses pettiness or when we justify our right to our emotional reactions or mental preoccupations, then we are turning our backs on True Source, turning away from the complete Love that True Source has for us, and for every being.

When our heart realizes this, then this effortless connection can be maintained for longer and longer periods and eventually becomes our spiritual normality. *'Abnormal' becomes the state of choosing our ego's preoccupations over the experience of True Source's Love.*

As we enjoy our spiritual connection allowing our hearts to accept True Source's Love, then The Love continues to cleanse our heart as we go about our day. This happens every moment, even while we are sleeping. We can awaken in the middle of the night and realize that the gentleness of True Source's Love is still radiating and giving us the best. Our hearts become free to be instruments continuously, during our waking and sleeping, for each moment we are enjoying True Source's Love gently radiating in all directions. *The core of our heart realizes that this natural experience of spiritual normality is easily achievable and closer than our minds can imagine. When our priority is set to choose The Love above all things, then The Love helps us get on with the process of dissolving what is not of The Love. Then this natural spiritual normality can become our innate state of being.*

Chapter 36
It is a Special Time to Be on Earth

The core of our heart realizes that this time in which we are now living is a very special time to be alive, that it is a great gift to be here on Earth. The reason for this is that now, we all have an opportunity for accelerated spiritual evolution far greater than we have ever had before. To our minds, this may not make sense because it may be said that we have always had the opportunity for spiritual growth or enlightenment. On one level this is true, but the difference regarding our present time is the profound ease with which we allow The Love to open our hearts, free from the typical resistance we faced in the past. Possibly the best way for me to explain the acceleration, in terms of the progressive ease with which we may now access and experience our spiritual hearts, is to share some personal historical perspective.

From 1974 to 2002 I had the opportunity to practice and teach different meditation systems. I practiced them as the 'doer' in charge of the process. For example, it was easy to be in the space between my thoughts and breaths and it was easy to feel how energy followed my intention. Learning to be the witness and feeling a deep stillness in my mind was simple to do. However, it was my mind that experienced the benefits. I was so proud of what I thought was my spiritual achievement. I thought I was a spiritual warrior who was cultivating my mind, and perfecting my ability to rise above it all. As I now realize, this was not the same as trusting, accepting and letting The Love open my non-physical heart.

This special time to be on Earth is directly related to our letting The Love of True Source open our spiritual heart. In the past, we have confused spiritual growth with the cultivation of our mind and the development of our soul.

When we feel our souls becoming stronger, becoming more enriched, it is so easy to convince ourselves that we are on the correct path. Why does this happen? The reason is because our soul, while under the influence of the ego, enjoys a quality of personal power characterized by feelings and thoughts such as, "I know, therefore I am," which may produce a heightened experience. Or it may assert the belief that, "It is my right to do what I choose to do." Another example would be thinking that 'I am that I am' is spiritual. These feelings create a predicament, because the soul adopts an attitude that keeps us separated from The Love. We become self-absorbed, relating to life as if it is 'us' that truly matters. The nature of this special time to be on Earth is not about our individual development or our personal advancement. It is about a collective spiritual flow that is in process and this flow is related to the core of the heart of every being. And most of all, it is about the complete Love that True Source has for every being on this dimension and all non-physical dimensions.

There are many who know this is a special time to be on Earth, but their concept of this 'specialness' is limited. They think this exceptional time is simply an opportunity for the soul to ascend to a higher dimension. However, the core of our heart contains the spark of Love and Light, our true essence, and the nature of our spiritual heart, and our divine connection to True Source, our Creator, is beyond all dimensions. The eternal call is not the call for our soul to ascend to a higher dimension. The core of our heart realizes that this particular call is the attraction beyond all attractions, our spark longing to reunite and become a part of The Love of True Source, again. What makes this time on Earth so special? Every day, more and more of us are beginning to respond to that 'Special Eternal Call' that is gently resounding throughout all of Existence.

As I have already shared, our soul was not created to exist for the fulfilment of its own agenda. Our soul was a gift from True Source, given to us as a facility to support the awakening of our spirit, our true self. The awakening of our spirit can only happen through the doorway of our spiritual heart. As we awaken, our spirit can learn and grow (true spiritual growth) while our soul and physical body allow us to have a form and learn lessons on the Earth dimension. Our ultimate lesson is learning to be grateful, to trust, feel, accept and choose True Source's Love above our right to be independent agents, living in separation and wandering through the universe fulfilling our ego's own agenda. To fully embrace this special time in Existence, it is crucial that we realize this from the depths of our heart, so we can be grateful for, and willing to feel and accept, True Source's complete

Love.

Around the year 2000 I came to realize that our non-physical heart was the key to spiritual fulfilment. I thought I was experiencing a direct connection to my heart, but I came to realize that what I was doing was very shallow and only barely scratching the surface of my heart. I even taught meditation and stress management workshops which focused on our heart as our true center, even though my understanding and experience of the heart was so very limited at that time. During this period, my whole approach to experiencing the heart was that it was up to us to make it happen, that we were responsible, that we were the 'doer' in charge of experiencing our heart. I did not realize then that only The Love of True Source could bring us into the deep experience of our hearts. I knew that our heart was the key, but the way that I approached the path of opening the heart did not allow me to be properly receptive to all the blessings that were being offered during this special time on Earth. I was still acting like the one responsible for my progress because I did not realize or have any experience of what it meant to truly rely on The Love instead of relying on my effort, methods or intentions.

In 2002 I was introduced to the Padmacahaya Foundation that operated under the guidance of Irmansyah Effendi, and I became a student of the Padmacahaya curriculum. At that time, for most participants in the workshops, opening the spiritual heart was a great challenge. We could easily sense the boundaries or edges of our non-physical hearts. As soon as we would relax and feel the beauty of our hearts, there would be a strong pressure inside our chests. Our hearts were very tightly bound and the non-physical boundary of the heart felt very fixed. As The Love within our heart radiated outward, it hit up against the boundary of the heart as if it had pushed up against a wall that did not want to budge.

During this period, it was common for people to feel nausea from this internal pressure and sometimes some of us would even vomit. This happened as we relaxed and began to let go of our inner observer and the domination of our heads. This was a challenging phase because, the moment we started to feel our hearts, we would float back up into our minds and shift back into our observer mode. We could not sustain the feeling of being connected to the spiritual heart. Feeling our hearts felt like trying to hold a ball under the water. If you let the ball go, it would just pop back up to the top. As soon as we felt our hearts, we would pop back up to our heads, back to being dominated by our ego consciousness.

As we let The Love bring us into our hearts, the pressure and uncomfortable sensations we felt in our chests were obvious. The more we cooperated with The Love, letting go of the observer quality of our minds and letting go of our effort and trying, the more our hearts became dominant. The more we let go, the pressure in our non-physical heart would begin intensifying because we were in reality holding back the flow of The Love. True Source's Love was ready to remove what was not of The Love, even though we were hesitant and resisting the process.

Another stage we went through included uncontrollable laughter that erupted from our hearts and could last for hours at a time. This intense gut-wrenching laughter was not based on something that was funny and it was not something we tried to make happen. The laughter was a cleansing on a deep heart level. It felt like laughter was a vehicle for True Source's Love to break through non-physical adhesions in the boundaries of our heart. It allowed the non-physical boundaries of our hearts to open and become more pliable.

Many of us experienced this intense stage. Those that resisted the uncontrollable laughing often did so because of their fear of letting go and fear of losing control. I could understand that very well. I felt that same fear, holding on to the view that I considered myself to be controlled and reserved in how I expressed myself. I remember feeling something strong that wanted to burst out from my heart and I held it back in mortal fear. As I held it back, the pressure gently intensified until I was willing to let go of control. Following some of these near peeing-in-your-pants laughing episodes that lasted at times for many hours, I could feel the boundaries and edges of my non-physical heart softening and I could feel that my heart was expanding bigger than my body. Along with others, I experienced that after The Love opened the heart, I would form new boundaries and edges in my non-physical heart. At times the pressure was very intense and we felt challenged by the levels of personal resistance we were facing.

Rather than feeling grateful, realizing that the pressure was only due to our blockages that had surfaced for cleansing, we sometimes chose to shut down the process of cleansing by returning to ego-based consciousness with our heads and our being observant fully intact. When we did this, the pressure went away because the cleansing process stopped.

It was, and is an unfolding process for us to realize that when our blockages surface, they are a gift and spiritual opportunity arising to help us face our emerging shadow. True Source's Love is always giving us the best of the best, always the most gentle and The Love would never harm us. When we feel pressure in our hearts, it is an indication that we are resisting The Love, not allowing The Love to remove what is not of The Love. As we let go of our being the doer, of our trying and observing, our hearts get cleansed and become more dominant. We do not have to suffer, because the radiating Love of True Source dissolves all our karmic blockages. As the blockages in our heart dissolve, our hearts are healed and become free to be instruments according to True Source's Love and Will. This is all part of the process of returning to spiritual wholeness.

In order to grow a healthy garden, the hard soil has to be tilled so that seeds can sprout and grow. Similarly, in 2003 and 2004, when we were letting The Love bring us into our hearts, our experiences continued to be very extreme. Our hearts were stubborn and the tilling of them was met with resistance. We were holding on to old patterns for dear life. Many negative emotions were surfacing with intensity, such as anger, fear, doubt or sadness. It was very difficult for any of us to feel the sublime gentleness of True Source's Love. At that time, our heart opening experiences were filled with tremendous sensations and surges of strong energy, or emotion.

When those strong emotions such as hurt or anger surfaced, they were not new emotions being created. They were old emotional blockages coming to the surface to be cleansed and dissolved forever. Even though the laughter helped many of us to clear them out, the cleansing experience continued to be very intense.

Then, I began to notice that by the time people began taking Open Heart Workshops in 2005, they still had cleansing reactions, but the intensity of the emotions that surfaced or the intensity of the uncomfortable pressure they felt in their hearts was significantly less than what many of us had gone through in 2002 and 2003. Letting go of trying or observing became much easier for the workshop participants to experience. It became a much gentler process as the new participants let go, and began to allow True Source's Love to open their spiritual heart.

Today, the ease involved in experiencing our spiritual hearts continues to progress and accelerate at an amazing speed. This is evident from the responses that participants share when I am teaching Open Heart Workshops. Their hearts are able to more easily feel, enjoy, trust and accept True Source's Love in a way that was so much more challenging for us just a few years earlier. True Source's

Love is cleansing and opening their hearts and The Love is dissolving the blockages easily without them having strong cleansing reactions. Participants also typically no longer go through the stage of deep laughter to open the boundaries of their hearts.

In a short period of time, workshop participants are now able to experience what previously took participants years to achieve. What is even more remarkable to me is that I have seen how everyday people from all walks of life are able to easily feel the peace, calmness and joy of their spiritual hearts with just some simple guiding: relaxing, smiling, and letting go of any personal sense of trying, effort, or observing. They do not feel the pressure or extreme cleansing reactions that people used to experience when they began to open their hearts in 2002.

As a psychologist, one part of my practice is to consult in nursing homes where residents are in the last chapters of their lives. It has been wonderful to experience the ease with which so many of these senior citizens are now able to learn to enjoy their spiritual hearts while feeling deeply grateful. They are often able to have moving heartfelt experiences during the first session in which they are guided to feel their hearts. In contrast, ten years ago, clients were not able to have these moving experiences in the same way. In fact, even just quieting their chattering mind was considered a big accomplishment. It is obvious from my work with a diversity of populations, that as time continues to unfold, enjoying the beauty of our hearts is getting easier and easier for those who are willing to 'stop doing' and to simply 'feel' what is present.

Today, those who continue on the spiritual path of opening the heart feel that their spiritual evolution is unfolding. As True Source's Love brings us deeper and deeper into our hearts we are joyfully letting The Love dissolve our blockages without resisting the process. It continues to become easier for the boundaries of our non-physical spiritual heart to keep expanding.

As our hearts continue to open, as our boundaries continue to dissolve, The Love within our hearts radiates without limit in every direction, and we enjoy the deeper experience of being an instrument of Love and Light for all beings.

Why is it getting easier for hearts to open? There appear to be two main reasons why this shift in spiritual consciousness is happening at an accelerated rate. *The first is that, as True Source's Love and Light gently radiates, moving through all dimensions including the Earth, more and more of us are letting The Love in, opening our hearts, and letting The Love cleanse our hearts. It is as if within our hearts, the glue binding together old and rigid patterns is dissolving. It is becoming easier to let go of blockages and patterns that do not serve us. Without holding on for 'dear life', it is easier to let go of our ego-patterns. Our hearts are waking up and hearing the call of True Source's Love.*

For many of us, we are not conscious of this positive shift. In time I trust it will become a more conscious experience. It will become clearer and clearer that our spiritual hearts are intimately connected to True Source. This sacred connection will grow in the gentleness and sweetness of The Love. The longing, the magnetic attraction of our spark, our true essence, to reunite with our Creator, will continue to develop and strengthen with time. We are now in the special time that many indigenous cultures and spiritual traditions throughout the world have spoken of. The Love of True Source is drawing us all nearer and nearer. *The core of our hearts knows it is time for everyone to come Home to who we truly are.*

The second reason for this shift in spiritual consciousness is that, rather than feeling separate from one another, functioning as individuals, we now have a growing feeling that we are all connected, spirit to spirit, and heart to heart, and that we are collectively moving together. Not that long ago, it was unheard of for a person to run a mile in less than four minutes. As soon as that first person broke through the four-minute barrier, it opened up a door and became so much easier for others to follow. There are now many people who have been able to break the four-minute mile. Similarly, as more hearts open, the doorway is opened for others to readily follow.

The spiritual journey is not about individually reaching the top of the mountain to achieve an enlightened state. It is not about any one of us getting spiritually 'ahead.' There is a collective spiritual flow that is gaining momentum now. Knowingly or unknowingly, we are all moving together. And our choosing The Love, our accepting the invitation of the Eternal Call, is always the most gentle of experiences. True Source will never force us.

However, as the present spiritual shift continues to unfold, and more and more of us joyfully choose to embrace and accept The Love, there may be pressure if anyone resists the flow. Those resisting The Love, resisting the gifts of Love, may feel like they are trying to swim upstream against a strong current. The harder one swims against the current, the more challenging the struggle is.

Over time, as more and more of us become instruments of The

Love, radiating the Love and Light to everyone, the collective spiritual current of The Love will become stronger and the invitation to freely choose True Source's Love over our ego's agenda will become sweeter and more beautiful. It will become more difficult to resist. We can choose to relax and enjoy the spiritual ride while feeling deep gratitude and connection to True Source, or we can resist and maintain our right to exist in separation as an ego invested in its own agenda. Any pressure and resistance that will be felt if we choose the latter, remaining head-dominant and ego-strong, is meant to let us know that we are 'heading' in the wrong direction. This pressure is not a punishment. It is a gift of Love from the Source of Love, letting us know that our ego is in charge.

The Love and Light of True Source is waiting to give all of us the best of the best. To benefit from all of the gifts of The Love, we have to be willing to let our hearts feel grateful for what we are receiving. However, our special time on Earth is not just about receiving. It is about our precious opportunity to become instruments of True Source's Love and Light by sharing and letting The Love within our hearts be free to radiate to all beings, so that all beings without exception are touched by The Love.

Chapter 37
The Time is Now

It is so easy for us to take time for granted. And it is so simple to forget that our days on Earth are numbered. We live as if there will always be a tomorrow and that we will always continue to wake up in the morning. We live, driven by our ego's agendas, our head-centered consciousness, continuously asking, "What's next?" The main point is that, spiritually speaking, life is precious and it is a most special and important time to be incarnated on Earth. Many of us can feel this very clearly.

Historically speaking, opening our non-physical spiritual heart just an inch was considered great spiritual progress. Now, so many people are allowing their spiritual hearts to open more. We are beginning to allow The Love to give us the best. Yet many of us do not yet fully appreciate how profound this is. It is not 'us' that opens our heart. When we 'feel' the beauty, blessings and The Love in our hearts, we give permission to The Love, and invite The Love to begin opening our heart.

It happens when we experience 'follow the feeling', and not through our 'doing,' that we allow True Source's Love to continue to flow and dissolve the blockages that keep us in separation. It is our heart's 'feeling' that is the language of our communication with The Love. This 'feeling' is not the same as the experience of emotion. 'Feeling' with the spiritual heart is the experience of sensing, enjoying and accepting The Love with gratitude and it is this 'feeling' that communicates to True Source that we are willing participants, and that we want to receive more and more of The Love. By using our hearts properly, as we 'follow the feeling' properly, we are learning to 'rely' on The Love above all things and allowing the process of our heart opening to unfold. The Love will never force us because forcing is against the nature of The Love. The Love only invites us to enjoy The Love within our hearts. 'Feeling' this gentle Love with our whole heart is the way in which we give permission to True Source to let The Love completely Love us. And as long as we continue to 'feel,' The Love will continue to flow.

Even though we may think that we know what it means to 'rely' on The Love, to some degree we are still relying on 'us.' There are deeper and deeper experiences of 'relying' on The Love. What stops us from further spiritual development is our reliance on our old ways and methods and our lack of trust in The Love. It was painful when I came to realize my arrogance in thinking that 'my ways,' 'my efforts,' 'my determination,' and 'my intention' would help me reach the highest spiritual goal. It was painful when I realized that I had been thinking that 'I' could do more for my spiritual evolution than what True Source, the Source of Love and Light, the Source that created the whole existence, could do.

For so long, I failed to realize that only True Source's Love could give the best of the best, beyond anything I could do when I was in charge, or by my being the 'doer', or using 'my methods' or best intentions. *True Source's Love is the best. True Source's Love is complete, and The Love is waiting to give the best of the best to every being. As we realize this, and we let our hearts open to this process, accepting The Love, letting The Love gently penetrate into the deeper levels of our heart, we finally realize our search is over. What we have been waiting for, from the very distant past to the present, is here and now. Now is the time for us to allow The Love of True Source to complete the process of bringing us back to where we belong.*

At the beginning of Chapter 1 you were invited to ask yourself the following questions: "Are you seeking enlightenment, salvation, yoga or, are you seeking to understand the deeper purpose of your life? Do you know what 'the deeper purpose of your life' means and how will you know it when you find it?" I invited you to also ask the question, "What is the meaning of spiritual growth and what determines true spiritual development?" It is my sincere hope that this book has helped you to gain new insights about the meaning and purpose of your life and helped you to understand what our spiritual journey is really all about. I felt inspired to write this book because my journey led me to realize that the different systems and approaches to spiritual growth that I had followed in the past were not truly supporting the opening of my spiritual heart.

Many of us have invested a lot of time and energy into a particular spiritual approach or paradigm and it may have once served us. Now, we may find ourselves at a juncture, searching again, because we realize that our old ways were limited and did not really satisfy us, or help us to open our heart.

It is not easy to let go of an approach to which we are committed. However, if we realize that our commitments served as stepping stones to bring us to this special moment in time, then it is easier to let go of our old ways with joy.

As I have shared throughout this book, true spiritual progress is not something we attain by 'our' effort or doing. It is not about perfecting mindfulness, mastering our ability to use intention, or 'our' mastering any meditation technique. Neither is the spiritual journey about climbing a mountain or striving for something far beyond our reach. Enlightenment is not about knowing it all, or our being able to manifest, or co-create our dreams, develop our souls, or learning to detach and rise above all life's challenges. We were not given this life for the purpose of our soul ascending to a higher dimension. It is not about the opening of our third eye, communicating with angels, using spirit guides, or relying on any intermediary, nor is it about meditating for extensive hours. Spiritual growth does not happen by 'our' being the 'doer' or because of our best intentions. It has nothing to do with proving our worthiness through practicing austerities or by our making great sacrifices.

Spiritual growth happens as a natural outcome, occurring when we whole-heartedly experience enjoying and accepting True Source's Love. Our spiritual growth happens as a result of our feeling grateful toward True Source, genuinely grateful, because we realize that only The Love of True Source can grow our spirit. And our progress only unfolds to the extent that we are willing to share the gentleness of True Source's Love that is radiating from our hearts.

I offer my apologies if my directness in this book has offended anyone's spiritual view, understanding, or paradigm. It felt important for me to express my realization that there are *not* a lot of 'options' when it comes to true spiritual growth.

As we begin to open our spiritual hearts properly, and begin to trust, accept and rely on The Love on deeper levels, it is normal for us to have feelings of inadequacy, hesitancy, resistance, and even fear, because, as we experience The Love giving us the best, the ego and soul may feel that it will lose control or fail to exist. We easily come up with reasons and excuses to maintain our separation as independent beings.

The good news is that, as we surrender to The Love, all we really lose or give up are our karmic blockages, our unresolved issues, our rights to be judgemental and all the excuses we use to become emotionally reactive. Do we really want to resist letting go of all that? This is not something to resist. Especially when we consider that trusting and relying solely upon True Source leads us to experience blissful freedom from our self-created dramas.

As we learn to rely on The Love, we also feel safer, and it is easier to let go of our edges and boundaries. They have kept us isolated from becoming a part of The Love. As our whole heart and whole being begins to trust The Love on deeper and deeper levels, we realize it is our joy beyond joys; that loving and trusting True Source is what our true self has been waiting for since time began. Our spiritual journey is designed to fulfil the purpose of why we exist. The spark of Love and Light in the core of our hearts, our true essence, is so very grateful to remember this again, so grateful to once again feel and hear the eternal call for our spirit, our true self to return Home; so grateful to have the opportunity to respond to this eternal call, to follow the 'feeling' in our heart, to become an instrument, and to become a part of The Love; so grateful to never again be separated from the complete Love True Source has for every being.

I trust that, after reading this book, you have a better understanding of the real difference between our spirit and our soul. We are a spirit, and our true essence is a spark from The Source. It is correct that our soul is a beautiful gift from True Source, but it is not who we are. Our soul was given to us to serve as an intermediate consciousness, a bridge between spirit and this material plane, so that our true self can learn on the Earth dimension. *The soul is meant to function as a humble facility to support the awakening of our true self.*

Our heart is the doorway because only with the core of our heart, are we able to feel the direct connection with True Source. When our multidirectional heart opens by accepting and enjoying True Source's Love, our spirit grows. Total credit needs to be given where credit is due. Only The Love of True Source grows our spirit, not 'us.' The very quality of our gratitude to True Source and the openness of our spiritual heart is a mirror of our spiritual evolution. In other words, the spiritual development of our true self is a direct reflection of the quality of our heart.

If our heart is truly able to feel a direct connection with our Creator, it will become obviously clear to the core of our being that placing anyone between us and True Source, or giving our worship/

adoration to any intermediary, will stifle the growth of our spirit. Our potential for the most direct and sacred relationship with our One and Only Creator will be limited. It would be like a child asking someone to speak to his mother and father instead of feeling safe enough to have a direct communication with them. True Source is inviting us to open our hearts and feel the beautiful enjoyable direct connection that is our birthright. For the True Parent of every being in the whole existence, every child matters, no matter what anyone has ever done in the past.

This spiritual journey is so simple; a joyful experience based on the direct loving relationship between our spark and our Creator. This journey is a process that allows The Love and Will of True Source to bring our true self back Home, restoring our true self to its original nature. This journey of our spirit, returning Home to True Source, fulfils the purpose of this life, and is the reason why we exist within Existence.

We are all siblings and children of True Source and on a spiritual level we are all connected. As more and more of us allow The Love to do whatever The Love wants to do with us, to cleanse and to dissolve all the blockages in our being that are not of The Love, then it will become easier and easier for everyone to enjoy their spiritual hearts.

Our individual healing is linked to the collective healing of all our hearts. The time is now for us to let True Source's Love and Will have its way, so that we can continue to collectively flow together. Then all of our true selves can awaken. It is time for us to become instruments of True Source's Love and Light, joyfully radiating the gentleness of The Love to all beings on every dimension in the whole existence. And it is time for our hearts to realize that only True Source's Love can set us free so we can fulfil the purpose of why we exist.

Summary
One Hundred Highlights

B elow is a summary of the main highlights I felt to share with you in this book. This may serve as a future reference for reviewing the main essence and principles. If you read these points simply as concepts to be digested by your brain, your understanding of them will be limited. If you read them for your heart to hear and feel, you may find that they may resonate and touch a deeper part of you as you gain insights into their true meaning. The reason is that you will most likely feel that many of these highlights ring true to your heart. But they may not ring true, or may even be met with resistance, by your mind. You can also benefit if you pause after each highlight and let them sink in, so you are feeling the deeper meaning they represent, rather than simply thinking about them. They are 'food' for heart.

1. There is a Source, The Source of Love and Light, The Source of everyone's true self. Who we really are is our true self, our spirit. Our heart is the key to our connection with True Source because the spark of Love and Light lives within the core of our spiritual heart. Only with our spiritual hearts can we properly feel the Complete Love True Source has for us, and, as we begin to use our hearts properly, following this feeling, we embrace and accept The Love, learn to trust The Love, find true joy, and truly fulfill the purpose of this life.

2. True Source has Complete Love for each and every one of us, and continuously, in each and every moment. Never for one moment has True Source ever abandoned or rejected us. The Source of Love and Light is not capable of harm and wants to give us the best of the best in every moment. If we feel ourselves having some resistance to this statement, perhaps it is because we are still holding on to feelings of abandonment,

betrayal or rejection left over from long, long ago. These un-resolved matters influence the way we relate to True Source. When our spiritual heart opens more and more, it becomes obvious that True Source has never rejected us. It is we who have rejected True Source's Love by choosing name, fame, power, control, expectations, desires, personal will, self-centeredness, unworthiness, or emotional reactivity over The Love.

3. The true longing, the deepest feeling in the core of our true self, is to return Home to The Source from which it came. The way of the spiritual heart, our true spiritual journey, is the journey of our spirit, our true self, returning Home to True Source's Complete Love. Only our inner heart, the core of our true self is pure. Our true self is in a state of incompleteness, and is still learning because it is living in separation. In isolation and sep-arateness, we have been suffering, never really finding satisfaction or true happiness. Our true and ultimate happiness comes in returning Home to the Source of Love and Light.

4. In order to provide the opportunity for our true self, our spirit, to return Home, True Source gave us the gift of a soul and heart so that we could incarnate and participate in existence for the sake of our spiritual evolution. Our soul's ability to create, manifest, and build its ranking in existence, is not why we exist. Our soul was designed by True Source to be a facility so that we can learn to choose, trust and accept The Love with our whole heart and whole being.

5. Our spirit learns and grows to the extent that we learn to choose True Sources Love above all things in our every moment on Earth. Our spirit grows when our heart opens bigger and bigger by feeling, enjoying and accepting The Love and Light of True Source. This is the spiritual process by which we become authentically closer and closer to True Source.

6. The spiritual journey is not about how good we are, how many great deeds we perform or how good we can become. It's not about all the magnificent things we do or how wonderfully we have developed our personal creativity and our ability to mani-fest our dreams. Neither is it about how bright we can shine. This is all part of a big trap that is easy to fall into since it seems glamorous and can inflate our egos with feelings of righteous-ness. Real spiritual growth only happens when our hearts open by connecting to True Source's Love, and not by developing our personal soul or ego power. The true expression of spiritual

growth is the journey of our spirit, our true self, returning to our Source. It is not the journey of the soul to reach a higher dimension or even the highest heavens.

7. It is time for us to wake up from the illusion of what we have thought freedom to be. Knowingly, or unknowingly, we have conditioned a part of us to think that freedom is our right to live independently, to do what we want, to have what we want and to manifest our dreams. This definition of freedom fulfills the delights of the soul but does not allow the true nature and freedom of our spirit to grow. Spiritual freedom is related to our non-physical heart being free from all blockages, in all its layers and in all its directions. It is the freedom of no longer being triggered, having no issues with anyone, anywhere, including from anything that ever happened at any time in our soul's journey. Then our heart is completely free to be an instrument of True Source's Love and Light. This is the freedom that our heart longs for which only The Love can give. Thinking that we can obtain freedom by other means is an illusion that we have been carrying since before the beginning of time.

8. True Source has complete Love for you, me and everyone, and it is our birthright, the right of every spark, to have direct access to this Divine Connection. To settle for anything less is missing what is most important in the whole existence. Existence was created to facilitate our heart getting back into a direct connection with our Creator so our spirit can fully awaken. It is easy for us to fool ourselves into thinking that there is some other purpose for our existence, and something else more important than True Source's complete Love for every being.

9. The best way to learn to rely on the Love completely is to accept True Source's invitation to become an instrument of The Love. By being an instrument, we become so grateful, as the Love and Light is radiating, in every direction, from our whole heart and whole being. We are so grateful for the opportunity to share The Love and Light, so that The Love can touch every being, everything and every event in existence. As we begin to trust, accept, feel and share The Love, we truly begin our spiritual journey, joyfully fulfilling our deepest purpose for being on this Earth.

10. We all have the same primary assignment. We are here to be instruments of True Source's Love and Light. Whatever we do in the world, whatever projects we take on, are secondary to our true purpose on Earth. The more we feel, enjoy and accept True

Source's Love, the sweeter and gentler True Source's Love is shared for the benefit of all beings. What a great arrangement True Source has given us! The more we enjoy True Source's Love, everyone benefits. As we allow The Love to radiate through us, we begin to let go of all our fears and limitations in sharing The Love with others. As we become sweeter instruments, we begin to let The Love impartially touch every being and every event in existence.

11. Only by our letting go of 'us', our 'I', letting go of all our trying and doing, all our observing, and relying solely, and completely, upon True Source's Love, can our spiritual heart be properly cleansed and purified, allowing our heart to open completely. We need to really understand that on our own, we cannot do anything to open our heart properly. We cannot use our 'I', we cannot do anything, and we cannot use any kind of effort, or use our desire, or our imagination, or use our mind in any way to open our heart. We cannot help. It simply does not work.

12. Knowingly or unknowingly, when our non-physical heart opens, it is The Love and Light from The Source of Love and Light that opens our heart. It is not our doing, efforts, special talents or ambitions. It is only by feeling and accepting The Love from The Source of Love and Light that our heart opens, allowing us to become who we are in the essence of our being.

13. The law of cause and effect is the law of karma. Every time 'we' act as the doer, every time we use our free will, we create karma. The seeds or imprints of our actions, our karmas, are stored in our heart and soul and, as they accumulate over time, they become blockages in the heart. A blockage in the field of our heart is anything that keeps True Source's Love from radiating sweetly, gently and completely to every being, in every direction, on every dimension in the whole existence. Blockages are only present because they exist in separation from The Love. True Source never wants us to be separate from The Love and wants to dissolve all of the obstacles we have accumulated.

14. The Law of Karma is a gift from True Source to help us learn to choose True Source's Way and True Source's Love above our ego's ways and the drive of our soul. It is through this learning process that our spirit, our true self, is awakened and grows to become a part of True Source's Love. Only then can we come Home to who we truly are. There is no other way out of the maze in which we have been wandering for a very, very, long time.

15. Living separated from True Source's Love as an independent being with our ego in charge is the most extreme type of suffering. We only begin to realize this when we let True Source's Love bring us into the depth of our hearts. Then when we leave our hearts and return to our ego's domain, we feel the pain of separation, and we realize the pain of separation has enslaved and kept us in prison. Yet we have acclimated to the state of separation, of suffering, and have come to view it as our normality.

16. True Source's Love is above the law of karma, and The Love does not want us to suffer. We may not realize what a Blessing this is. What does it mean that True Source's Love is above the law of karma? It means that when we let The Love bring us into our hearts, then The Love effortlessly dissolves all our karmic seeds and all our deep inner blockages. We experience no karmic suffering, because the seeds of our karmas from the long journey of our soul are dissolved and will never have the opportunity to ripen. When we rely on The Love and let The Love be the doer, we stop creating more blockages or seeds of karma in the soul and the heart. We simply let The Love remove that which is keeping us separated from The Love so that we can spiritually grow and fulfill our true nature, our true purpose.

17. The only thing that is supposed to be in our heart is the radiance of True Source's Love and Light. All our karmas, or 'sins,' are energy blockages we accumulate when we live as an ego stuck in our heads and separated from The Love. Simply having the thought, or believing in any savior, does not dissolve the accumulation of all blockages. This type of belief only comforts the mind. Someone believing may feel assured that death will result in a permanent place in heaven. Salvation is only salvation when the heart is completely free. Just because we believe our heart is free does not mean that all issues and blockages are dissolved. The extent to which we have no issues with anyone, anywhere, on any dimension reflects the extent to which our heart is free, free to allow for the gentleness of True Source's Love to radiate. The radiation of True Source's Love then flows sweetly and freely to the heart of every being in the whole existence without any resistance. Until then, we still have karma or what may be understood as the 'sin' of separation from Love.

18. When we follow our old ways, we continue to strengthen our separation from The Love. Our ego becomes stronger and stronger. The use of our free will to do things according to our wants,

hopes and desires continues to spin a karmic web around us. Of course, True Source has complete Love for every being, and The Love is always present waiting to give us the best. In the core of our hearts, we know that it is time for us to come into alignment with the bigger picture. The great plan is to become instruments of True Source and to enjoy with abundant gratitude, the gentleness of The Love radiating to the hearts of all beings.

19. If our accomplishments lead us to realize the limitation of living for the sole purpose of fulfilling our needs, dreams, hopes and expectations, then truly we are ready to wake up from our worldly slumber. If we do not come to this realization, the illusion of achieving and gathering more can drive us to our last breath.

20. Our heart develops blockages from the emotional reactivity experienced when our ego and mind are in charge of the show. We do not contaminate the field of our non-physical heart when we are living our life from within our heart. The real problem is not that we have a mind. Remember, our soul, mind, brain and physical form were given as a gift by True Source, as vehicles to help facilitate our heart to open and for our true self to finally awaken. The problem occurs when we let the ego be the director. When the brain and mind are dominant, the heart remains closed. We are disconnected from our greatest gift and treasure given to us, our hearts.

21. When we allow The Love to open our hearts by accepting and trusting the Source of Love and Light, the heart invites the brain to become a friend in the service of helping us carry out the orders of our heart. We make positive choices and feel good at the same time. Then, even though we are using our brain, we don't create resentments or fears. We do not contaminate the field of our heart when we are operating from within our heart. We only contaminate the field of our heart when our brain is dominant and our ego is running the show.

22. We were not created to be a 'doer' or to be a 'co-creator'. We were created to enjoy being Loved by True Source and to share The Love. We do not exist so that we can continue expressing and developing our right to be independent and separate from The Love. We exist so that we can learn to let True Source's Love bring us back to where we belong. With that understanding, it is very arrogant for us to think that we know a better way than what True Source, the Source of all of Creation, can do for us. It is time for us to let True Source's Love do what The Love

wants to do, and that is to remove all of our suffering, recent and ancient blockages, and to end the pain of our separation.

23. It is important for us to realize that our emotional reactions are not absolute fact. These reactions are the story line of the personal soap opera we create in any given moment based on how our brain is reacting, or how our emotions are being triggered in that moment. We believe it is real but it is just a story created in the world of our mind.

24. We do not realize the extent of our fear, guilt, shame, unworthiness, or anger. We do not realize the extent of our wounds, traumas, resentments and unforgiving attitudes toward ourselves and others. Those with whom we find fault are actually our teachers because they help us to recognize our patterns of judgment, arrogance and self-righteousness. Those with whom we find fault are also our teachers because our judgmental reactions show us the ways we choose to be separate from The Love.

25. The ego acts as if there is a ladder which it is climbing to get somewhere. But it is a ladder to nowhere that continues to engage us, to keep us in our busyness, and to guarantee our existence as an isolated being. In the core of the heart, every heart is longing to never again be separated from True Source's Love. Yet when we live our life as if our ego is striving to get 'somewhere', we will never really truly arrive. The reason is that there will always be a sense of taking the next step on the ladder and this impulse is what drives our mind. Our ego has created so many ways to continue justifying our experience of living in separation.

26. Our heart relationship with True Source is the only relationship that is truly safe and where it is totally advisable to let go of all boundaries. When we begin to experience the heart, we realize that we create boundaries or have edges in place. The ways in which we have created these edges are related to our past pain from interpersonal relationships and most importantly, the way we have learned to stay separate from The Love. Dissolving the boundaries of our non-physical multidirectional heart happens when we let go of our defensive armor. This armor is the means we use to protect our definition of who we think we are. We create armor because we fear what will happen if we allow ourselves to be loved completely.

27. All True Source wants to do is to Love you, me and everyone completely in every moment... always, and far beyond what our brain or ego can ever imagine. Our boundary is our resistance to letting True Source Love us the way The Love is intended to do. When our heart begins to feel, enjoy, trust and accept True Source's Love, the non-physical boundary of our spiritual heart begins to open and expand. As we let The Love give us the best, then The Love begins to set our heart free. This is the direction of the true freedom that the core of every heart knowingly or unknowingly seeks.

28. When we allow The Love to help us trust, enjoy and accept True Source's Love with complete gratitude, then The Love will dissolve everything that is not of The Love. We will have no issues with anyone, anywhere on any dimension, and our heart will be free to let True Source's Love and Light radiate to the heart of every being in the whole existence without exception. This is the essence of what it truly means to experience forgiveness at the deepest level.

29. We can use our free will to remain separate from The Love or we can use it to choose to embrace and accept True Source's Love. The greatest choice we can make is when we use our free will to choose True Source's Love above all things. Making this choice is the most important thing we have to do in this life. When we use our free will to stay in separation, we remain as an independent agent addicted to our own agenda while we wander through existence chasing our hopes, wants and desires. And we can be in separation, with our own agenda, while thinking, while believing, that we are growing spiritually.

30. By feeling, trusting, enjoying and accepting True Source's Love with gratitude, we are open to letting The Love clean up the mess we created when our ego was in charge. True freedom is the freedom of our spark to never again be separated from True Source's Love. The core of our hearts realize what this means in a way that our ego or mental concepts could never conceive.

31. If we are honest with ourselves, we realize that a significant portion of our waking hours is spent engaging fragmented thoughts, living in our head, as we wander from past to future preoccupations or from one unsettled issue that triggers the next unsettled feeling. We put a make believe circle around the multiple fragments and expressions of the ego and say, "This is who I am." Then we move and act in the world as if we know

who we are. We defend our turf, our ways, habits, desires and concepts. We fail to realize that our ways, habits and unresolved issues tend to define and defend our ego and that keeps us in separation from The Love.

32. It is time for us to stop fooling ourselves, thinking, "We know best." It is important for us to realize that we like to do it 'our way' because we are afraid to trust The Love. Doing it our way helps us to avoid our fear of what will happen if we trust The Love completely. And our way is so limited yet we hold onto it with full rights of ownership. Only when our way becomes the way of True Source's Love can our spiritual journey unfold. Our hearts have to recognize this.

33. We are not on Earth to be a human being who expresses the complete range of our emotional experiences. We are here on Earth to learn to become who we really are; to become spiritual beings in a human form. Emotional reactivity and mental reactions are the ego's very good friends because they justify its right to be alive. The ego has perfected the art of using excuses and justifications. It does so to be able to maintain its right to feel what it feels and react the way it reacts.

34. It is important for us to realize that we are the ones who suffer from our emotional reactivity, because, at that time, we are choosing our right to be consumed by our ego's agenda over feeling True Source's Love. Our heart has to realize what it means to turn our back on True Source's Love. Whether we want to admit it or not, this is what we are doing when we follow our emotions, ways and ego habits.

35. Emotions do have a purpose and can be our friend if we use them as a teacher helping us realize those moments when we are disconnected from The Love. To fulfill our deepest purpose of existence, we have to let go of all our excuses that justify our right to become emotionally reactive. The ego maintains a hidden repertoire of strategies to continue its existence as an independent agent, and these emotional charges allow the ego to stay separate from The Love.

36. Life has a way of triggering and mirroring our unresolved blockages and issues by bringing them to the surface. That is what life is designed to do, so we can continue to have the opportunity to choose The Love above all things. By choosing The Love instead of our right to continue our patterns of emotional reac-

tivity, we allow The Love to dissolve and heal our wounded past.

37. When you learn to experience your heart, you realize that your head and heart can look at the same event in very different ways. Being in our head, we take things so much more personally. We tend to get defensive or protective of our positions. Your heart does not have an interest in taking things personally.

38. When the ego is in charge, there is a tendency to create a sense of a pecking order. Our heart has no interest in putting people down or judging them because the core of our heart knows that every human being is our sibling. The gift of our heart allows us to be patient and tolerant of imperfections in others in a way which our head does not. When we live from our heart, we are in a stable space, and we don't have to judge or compare ourselves to others. We can still form opinions, though our opinions do not have the emotional charge or arrogant flavor that is associated with judgments. From the perspective of our heart, we do not view or relate to life in terms of a pecking order.

39. By finding fault with others it allows us to feel more secure in our own position. If we are honest with ourselves, we realize that we have played this ego game on a number of occasions in our life. It gives us a false sense of security or worthiness. One gets to think they are more worthy because they have placed others below them. We do this when we judge each other. By finding fault in other people, it also helps us to feel more secure in our own sense of who we think we are. This pattern that the ego plays so well is linked to feelings of arrogance, righteousness or superiority.

40. The ego likes score cards so it can keep track of when it thinks we won or lost. The problem is that the purpose of life is not about winning or losing. The ego will keep us thinking that at any given moment, we are either getting ahead or getting behind. True spiritual growth has nothing to do with our personal score card, or how well we think we are doing, and it is not related to all the wonderful things we have done. It is time for us to let go of our score cards. The true spiritual journey is not about how good we can become. It is about our trusting and accepting The Love of True Source above all things, with abundant gratitude, each and every moment of our lives. This means we are willing to let The Love help us to let go of all our judgments toward ourselves and toward others. True spiritual progress can only be measured according to the quality, openness and condi-

tion of our heart and how well our hearts radiate The Love to every being in the whole existence.

41. When we have arrogance and think we are right, being right gets us a step up the illusionary ladder that leads to nowhere. Due to our arrogance, any step upward that an ego takes to be above another person, is a spiritual hindrance. It is important for us to learn to recognize the varied expressions arrogance can take as it easily slips into our everyday interactions, or dances in the privacy of our thoughts. These moments are cues to let us know we are not grounded in our spiritual hearts.

42. Excuses are one of the favorite foods for our ego. Excuses allow the ego to maintain its identity as a separated being that has the right to be angry, resentful, outraged, hurt, insecure, judgmental or aloof. It is often convenient to blame someone or something else for reasons why things in a given moment are not as good as they should be. This is a way we often use excuses to shift responsibility away from ourselves.

43. The different excuses for why we think we have a right to be emotionally reactive occur in so many shapes and forms. If we sincerely want to grow spiritually, we have to be willing to give up our excuses and justifications regarding our right to all of our emotional reactions. To give up our right to use excuses feels threatening to the ego, because if we give up our excuses, our ego will lose a significant amount of power to maintain itself as a separate and reactive being.

44. The ego finds it natural to judge and does so in both obvious and very subtle ways. The ways can seem so natural, that it can be difficult to recognize how frequently we are actually judging people or circumstances in our everyday lives. Judgment disguises itself in what we have come to think is normal, so we keep doing it over and over again without even realizing we are doing it. When we judge, arrogance or the illusion of spiritual superiority is not far around the corner. When we are truly in our heart, our heart does not judge because it is not capable or interested in doing so. It is important to note that disagreeing with someone's poor choices is not the same as judging them. When we disagree without judgment, we do not create any emotional charge or sense of superiority. We do not have the feeling of being above or below another and we simply let them be. When we let True Source's Love open our spiritual heart, we can enjoy our heart while giving the world permission to be imperfect.

45. How we respond when people do things we do not like or agree with is a mirror into ourselves. Any person or thing that pushes our buttons in any shape or form becomes our teacher or a facility for our spiritual growth. When we experience judgment, blame, or any expression of emotional reactivity, rather than focusing on the external trigger, it is important for us to recognize that we have resistance somewhere in our being. Rather than realizing that the key issue is the friction and that the resistance is within us, we tend to stay focused on the external trigger. Then, with our emotions on the trigger, we think we have a good excuse and reason to remain in a state of emotional reactivity.

46. This precious gift of life provides opportunities for our patterns to surface so we can learn to choose The Love above all things. When we feel, accept and enjoy the gentleness of True Source's Love, our blockages and ego patterns dissolve and our spiritual hearts begin to open more and more. Learning to choose True Source's Love above everything else is why we exist on Earth. This is the process of how our spirit, our true self awakens and grows to become a part of True Source's Love.

47. Often in the name of 'caring', we may become angry, outraged, disgruntled or upset. But emotional reactivity in the name of caring concern is a deception of the ego. This just adds more negative energy to an already challenging situation. Even if we think this form of 'caring' is helping, in actuality our emotional negativity is energetically polluting our hearts, our space and those around us. Being an instrument of True Source's Love and Light is the highest expression of our caring for others or about events and circumstances. It is important for us to be grateful for the opportunity to let True Source's Love and Light touch the heart of every being. Spiritual caring is the same as being an instrument, and this spiritual caring becomes the natural attitude of our heart when we begin to let The Love set our heart free.

48. It is time for us to begin opening to the experience of letting True Source Love us completely and continuously. This is what True Source wants to do so that all the wandering children in the desert can be brought Home to the joy of our true nature. And by feeling, enjoying and accepting True Source's Love with gratitude, we can then be instruments for True Source's Love to radiate to the hearts of all beings on all dimensions, everywhere. It is important for our heart to remember that this is the number one assignment we all share and the bigger purpose

of why we exist on Earth. When we are in True Source's Love and Light, there is no need to be concerned about defending or protecting ourselves. Relying upon the Love and letting The Love bring us into our hearts is the safest place to be.

49. We are not here on Earth to develop the greatness of our soul. That has been our distraction for eons, and it has only gotten us into deep karmic debt. Our soul and physical form were given as a gift from True Source for the purpose of our spirit, our true self to awaken. This awakening can only happen when we learn to rely on and let The Love open our hearts. As our hearts accept The Love of True Source, our spirit is able to grow. This is why it is referred to as 'spiritual growth.'

50. When a soul perceives itself as being in an elevated status, it functions as if its existence is a blessing to others. This soul's sense of greatness or higher dimensional status is actually its greatest spiritual hindrance. When we are being an instrument of True Source, we realize that we are not capable of blessing anyone. All the credit for the blessing is given to True Source. All blessings are experienced as a part of True Source's complete Love for every being. We are simply grateful to be a sweet child of our most beloved Creator. When a true self is awakening in The Love of True Source or has become a part of The Love, no aspect of their being is willing or interested in accepting worship energy. All credit is always given to the Perfect and Complete Love of the One and Only Creator. When The Love of True Source brings us closer to the experience of becoming a part of The Love, then we find that we are not capable of taking credit or ownership for anything. To take credit, we have to separate ourselves from The Love.

51. When we give another being our love and our power and place them in an intermediary position, we limit our spirit, our true self. This does not allow the core of our heart to have a direct connection with our Creator, our One and Only True Parent. True Source is waiting for us to let go of our old ways and habits, inviting us to have a direct connection to True Source's Love. The Love is always waiting and never compelling or forcing because The Love is gentler than gentle and softer than soft. This is a very important realization for our hearts. True Source is calling and waiting for us to trust The Love so we can have a direct connection with our Beloved Parent.

52. True Source has complete Love for you, me and everyone, and

it is our birthright, the right of every spark, to have direct access to this Divine Connection. To settle for anything less is missing what is most valuable in all of existence. Existence was created to facilitate our heart getting back into a direct connection with our Creator so that our spirit can fully awaken. It is easy for us to fool ourselves into thinking that there is some other purpose for our existence, and something else more important than True Source's complete Love for every being.

53. Our true purpose is not about what we can achieve, create, manifest, or how we can use our intention to influence life. Our soul and physical form are gifts meant to serve as a vehicle so we can take form on Earth for the purpose of our spiritual development. The purpose of the soul is not to exist for its own purpose, but for the soul to be a facility for fulfilling our spiritual destiny. Who we really are is not our soul. The essence of who we are, the spark of our true being that lives within the heart, is our spirit; this is our true self. Only when our heart accepts True Source's Love, can our heart open and grow. As our hearts open more and more, our spirit begins to shine and our true self awakens from its long slumber. It is only then that our true self is on its way Home, fulfilling the purpose, the true nature, of this life.

54. We have to realize that for so long we have been relying on 'us' as being the key, and really, if we are honest, we are still unhappy and still searching for happiness. Relying on us has never, nor will it ever work. Now is the time to properly learn to use our spiritual heart; to feel, embrace, accept, trust and rely on True Source's Love. Until we accept our own limitation to spiritually progress, we will not be able to allow The Love to help us so that we can receive the best of the best. When we learn to let The Love help our heart to feel, our heart naturally follows the feeling and trust grows. We then find ourselves relying more and more on True Source's Love and our spiritual connection deepens.

55. As we begin to accept and enjoy The Love, choosing The Love above all things and we will begin to experience and see life through different eyes. In addition to an inner calm, peace, light and joy, there will be a growing feeling of being loved completely, and that is something beyond our mind's capacity to compre-hend. We are here on Earth to become who we truly are, to be-come a spiritual being while enjoying the beauty of consciously

living as a child of the Creator.

56. If we do not rely directly on True Source's Love, then we become dependent on how good we think we can become. Only The Love of True Source is permanent. Whether or not we realize it, The Love of True Source is our lifeline and our refuge in the ocean of existence. True Source is the only Perfect One and The Love of True Source is the only Perfect Love. In order to be brought closer to True Source, our Creator and Source of our true self, our spirit, our spark, we must allow The Love to have its way with us. The Love can only have its way with us when we let The Love bring us into our hearts.

57. The nature of The Love is to dissolve everything that is not of The Love, not a part of The Love, so that The Love can set our hearts free. The observer of our consciousness has to submerge into the spiritual heart for us to be fully present as a heart. This happens when we let go of our ability to observe and allow True Source's Love to bring us into our hearts. Being within the heart properly, The Love can then begin to help and guide us to become proper instruments of The Love and Light for every heart in existence.

58. If we do not allow The Love to open our hearts, our true self does not awaken in the spirit of Love and Light. We may have the most impressive, powerful and magnanimous soul, but as the power of the soul grows, simultaneously our spirit is squelched. A powerful soul and a true self awakening in the sweet gentleness of True Source's Love cannot simultaneously exist. This is why many paths may seem as if they are helping us to spiritually grow, but they may be leading us down the limited path of soul development instead.

59. The irony is that the 'me' we know has never been who we really are in the first place. The reality is that we have been defending and protecting at all costs 'who we are not,' laboring under the illusion that we have been protecting ourself. We have forgotten the truth of who we really are, that we are sparks of Love from the Source of Love and Light. Failing to realize the blockages we have created, we continue to protect our right to be 'who we think we are.' And this has blinded us to who we truly are. We are children of True Source.

60. Heart intelligence guides us to make wise choices. It helps us to learn lessons that we were failing to learn when we were

stuck in our heads and falling into the same old holes. Heart intelligence helps us to perceive the bigger picture and develop greater clarity about situations and relationships. When True Source's Love radiating through our heart is strong, we will cringe at the idea of doing something that goes against our heart intelligence. But if the head is dominant, there is a chance that the ego can figure out a way to justify its actions. Even though the excuse or reason may be ridiculous, the ego is capable of believing it in order to act on behalf of its self-interests.

61. Following the heart can be tricky because sometimes we may think we are following our heart when we are really following emotions. When we are truly grounded in our heart, we are experiencing the gentleness of True Source's Love. This allows us to be in the position to make choices without an overlay of emotion. When emotions arise along with our hopes, desires and expectations, then we are not in a position to experience the wisdom of our hearts. Even though we think we are making a heart-centered choice, we may be making an emotional choice because our emotions have been activated. This is why we make poor choices and blame our hearts when actually we are making an emotional choice.

62. When we live with an open heart, remaining connected to our experience of True Source's Love, using our heart intelligence becomes a natural part of everyday life. The deepest experience of heart intelligence is the realization of our inner heart, which resides within the spiritual heart and is the very core, the essence of our true self. Since the inner heart is the direct spark of Love and Light from the Source of Love and Light, it is the only part of us that is completely pure. To feel the inner heart is to remember, to feel our longing to be reunited with True Source's Love.

63. When our hearts are open, we naturally and effortlessly maintain healthy interpersonal boundaries. We are able to accept differences, tolerate the imperfections of others, and not get pulled into drama. When a situation calls for us to be firm, we do so in a respectful way. We do it from a natural, heart-centered, neutral space that is free from judgment or charged emotional responses.

64. In any ordinary human relationship, it is important to have healthy boundaries. There is only one relationship in which it is safe to completely let go of our boundaries, and that is our

relationship with True Source. When we let The Love open our heart, dissolving our non-physical boundaries and edges, The Love is then free to remove all our blockages. To the degree that we trust, feel and accept True Source's Love with gratitude, the boundaries of our personal limitations dissolve. Our hearts open so that we can receive all the benefits of being cleansed by The Love while also having the blessed opportunity to be an instrument of True Source's Love and Light for all beings everywhere.

65. When grounded in our hearts, wonderful moments are not defined by what is going on in the external world. Moments are wonderful because of our heartfelt gratitude and connection to the complete Love True Source has for every being. This is why feeling our heart is the path to freedom. By following the heart, our happiness is no longer enslaved, or dependent on what is happening around us. We are happy whether or not we get our likes met or are able to avoid our dislikes.

66. When our joy is not based on external circumstances, we can break the chain that keeps us in the bondage of our work, chore and reward cycle. Our heart allows us to let go of the distinction of work and reward, and pleasure and pain. Everything that we do becomes enjoyable, even doing things that our ego previously despised. There can be no greater reward than The Love because True Source's Perfect Love is always giving us the best of the best, dissolving our blockages, and removing everything that is not of The Love. When our heart realizes what this means, our gratitude soars, becoming exponentially enhanced.

67. It is time for us to wake up from the illusion of what we have thought freedom to be. Knowingly, or unknowingly, we have conditioned a part of us to think that freedom is our right to live independently, to do what we want, to have what we want and to manifest our dreams. This definition of freedom fulfills the delights of the soul but does not allow the true nature and freedom of our spirit to grow. Spiritual freedom is related to our non-physical heart being free from all blockages, in all its layers and in all its directions. It is the freedom of no longer being triggered, having no issues with anyone, anywhere, including from anything that ever happened at any time in our soul's journey. Then our heart is completely free to be an instrument of True Source's Love and Light. This is the freedom that our heart longs for which only The Love can give. Thinking that we can

obtain freedom by other means is an illusion that we have been
carrying since before the beginning of time.

68. When our head is in charge, our heart and true self are in a
state of disconnect. Every moment we turn away, disconnected
from True Source's Love, we also deny True Source the opportunity to use us as an instrument of The Love and Light. Every
moment we choose to feel True Source's Love, we turn that
moment we are waiting on the grocery line into an experience
that our hearts can enjoy, be grateful for, all the while smiling to
the hearts around us, feeling True Source's Love radiating to the
hearts of all beings. In the simple acts of everyday life, we get to
participate in the great plan, allowing The Love to do just what
The Love wants to do... and that is, to radiate gently, sweetly
and freely, to all hearts everywhere.

69. Our multi-layered spiritual heart holds the entire spectrum of
our unresolved issues, unresolved emotions, un-forgiveness
toward others and ourselves, unresolved issues with God, guilt,
shame, unworthiness, anger, and many other blockages. The
conglomeration of all of these blockages in the different parts
of our non-physical heart tells the story of our past. It is all
linked to the collective karma of our soul's journey. All of our
issues and unresolved blockages are what keeps True Source's
Love from being able to use our heart as an instrument. And
since True Source's Love never wants us separate from The
Love, True Source's Love is always waiting to support us in dissolving everything that is not of The Love. Only when we let True
Source's Love dissolve everything that is not of The Love can
we become the children of True Source as we were designed to
be in the original blueprint. There is no one, including ourselves
who can do this for us. It is only by accepting and enjoying True
Source's Love with gratitude, that we allow The Love to engage
in the process of truly setting us free.

70. We strive to prove our worth, because we feel unworthy of True
Source's complete Love. In the core of our heart, we know that
approval from True Source is not needed because The Love is
present always and forever. We have never had to earn True
Source's Love. Yet, from our past journey, because our soul has
accumulated abandonment and rejection issues, we may feel
that we have to somehow prove ourselves, showing True Source
that we deserve to be Loved. The very core of our heart knows
that True Source never abandoned or rejected us. We are the

ones who turned away from The Love. If we ever think that True Source abandoned or rejected us, then, that is our projection.

71. Our heart condition and the willingness of our heart to be grateful, while feeling, enjoying and accepting True Source's Love reflects the degree to which we trust The Love. The core of our heart knows our spiritual worth is not performance-based. It is not about what we have done or what we will do. True Source's Love for us is unconditional. We are all worthy and deserving of True Source's complete Love, each and every moment, because True Source is our One and Only Parent and we are the children of True Source. When the core of our heart realizes that we have been loved completely, even during the darkest moments of our ancient past, we will never be the same again. In every moment, True Source's Love and Light is calling us Home to be who we are, to be as sparks which are no longer separated from The Love.

72. Death brings us back to our non-physical nature without the protective and insulative covering of our physical form. The overall experience, the vibration, the nature we had and expressed on Earth is amplified because there is no place to hide. If our heart was attuned to accepting and embracing The Love, then our experience of The Love and Light will be beyond anything we experienced on Earth because the experience is no longer filtered by the density of our physical form.

73. True Source's Love is present for every being, unconditionally Loving us and always giving us the best of the best, whether we are in physical or non-physical form. We are the ones who have the option, the choice, to run away, to hide in a dimmer place, because we are scared to embrace The Love and Light. True Source never sends anyone to a lower dimension. Souls go there of their own accord because, filled with shame or resentments, they do not feel comfortable with the brightness of The Love and Light. Dimmer dimensions are only temporary resting places. Because True Source has such complete and continuous Love for us, our life journey always presents us with opportunities to choose The Love over our soul and ego agendas.

74. The deepest purpose of our existence is for our true self or spirit to learn to be completely directed to our Creator and to accept, embrace and trust The Love above all things. Our soul and physical form have been given to us as gifts for learning on this physical dimension so that, who we are as a true self can

awaken within True Source's Love and Light. Our ultimate destiny is for our true self to return to our Source. Spiritual growth is the journey of our spirit, whose purpose is to return Home.

75. True Source does not punish anyone. The idea of a punishing God is a human mental construct. The core of our heart knows that the only relationship our Creator has with us is one of pure Love. True Source's complete Love is here in every moment. The opportunity, the pathway, is always present, every moment, for every being to return Home. We can remember again and become who we truly are: sparks of the Creator.

76. It is important for the core of our heart to realize that never, for one moment, has True Source ever abandoned or rejected us. It is we who fail to embrace and accept True Source's Love. We are the ones who misuse our free will and block True Source's Love from dissolving all of the karmic blockages from our ancient past. We have this life, this opportunity, to learn to use our free will to choose The Love and let True Source bring us out of ego separation and to once again become a part of The Love, never to be separated again.

77. When we examine our past history along with all our old patterns of emotional reactivity, the misconceptions we have held, as well as our projections, we better understand why we now have so much resistance to letting True Source Love us completely. We need to realize we are the ones who have not yet learned to truly accept True Source's complete Love, and not blame True Source, or fear True Source. Just as a loving mother is always available to hug her baby in need, True Source's Love is waiting for us to accept The Love, to feel the Love with our whole heart and our whole being. Only then can we let The Love cleanse our heart all the way to the core so that all that remains in the field of our hearts is the radiance of The Love and Light. Then our true self can awaken to its natural and original state and our soul can fulfill its function as a facility, and support the journey of our spirit, our true self, to return Home. Then on Earth, our multidirectional hearts can radiate True Source's Love and Light to everyone, sharing The Love as instruments in accordance with The Love and Will of True Source.

78. Living with an open heart is the safest way to live. Not doing so boils down to our lack of trust in our own heart, and our mistrust of The Love. Many of us fear that if we really let go and let The Love of True Source embrace us completely, then something

bad will happen. What if we lose our selves in the Love, or lose our existence or get out of control? In actuality, when we allow The Love to embrace us completely, what gets lost is who we are not. The Love only dissolves all of the aspects we created which have kept us in separation from The Love. The real you, you as a true self, can never be dissolved and will always be you.

79. When our heart realizes and begins to accept that True Source just wants to Love us completely in every moment, then our using other methods or techniques, like mantras, mindfulness, intention or anything that is not the direct connection with The Love, seems absurd.

80. We have turned our back on True Source's Love, and instead we have chosen the agenda of our own importance, ways, habits, and concepts. If we protect our agenda and even defend it at all costs, this choice can follow us to the grave and this life will have effectively been for naught. Yet we tend to protect and defend our right to our agenda because the ego continuously tricks us into believing that doing this is in our best interest. Choosing to follow the ego has sent us on a wild voyage through time, a journey that resulted in our gathering a karmic collection of blockages. These blockages burden our hearts, resulting in our living a life in which we are not free to fully enjoy, trust and accept True Source's Love.

81. In order to grow spiritually, we need to redefine our concept of freedom. Instead of defining freedom as being free to play how 'we' want to play, playing as an independent agent cruising through life, we understand that true freedom is found in the ultimate joy of not resisting the full expression of True Source's Love. We become truly freer as we enjoy, trust and accept True Source's Love with gratitude on deeper and deeper levels.

82. As we begin to trust, enjoy and accept True Source's Love, The Love gently dissolves our long-standing dysfunctional patterns and we change rapidly; at times even instantly. When we let True Source's Love give us the best by removing all our blockages and anything we are holding onto that is not of The Love, our purpose then comes into alignment with True Source's Purpose. The core of our heart knows this as truth and is waiting for our whole heart and whole being to join the bigger plan.

83. We act as if the car we are driving is stuck in the mud and we

think if we keep stepping on the gas it will get us out of the hole. When my heart realized how deep the karmic rut we collectively share is, and that all of our old ways and approaches have failed to get us out of the hole, it seemed ridiculous to continue on the path of 'me' being in charge of achieving spiritual progress!

84. Just because we think we are surrendering more and more, does not mean that we actually are. It is hard for us to understand the box that we are living within because we are contained in that box and confined by its walls. If we truly seek spiritual growth, it is time for us to let down our guard, our resistance and the ways in which we protect those walls. This is easier said than done because the part of us that may be thinking or believing that, "I am surrendering now" is contributing to the illusion that our 'I' is capable of or is actually interested in surrendering itself.

85. One reason that this spiritual journey is tricky is because we do not fully realize the extent to which we guard and resist the process of letting The Love give us the best. We may say the right words to ourselves such as, "I am ready to let The Love give me the best," and then, off we go, proceeding to be in charge of the process, as we attempt to supervise The Love. Knowingly or unknowingly, due to our lack of complete trust in The Love, there is a part of us that remains as a witness and observer of our experience, and this is the part of us that feels compelled to supervise the Love.

86. In actuality, being the mindful witnessing observer is a hindrance because we think that the observer is who we are. It is still just 'us' functioning as an independent entity separated from The Love. This mental observer is linked to our soul. It is important to remember, we do not exist to grow the stature of our soul. Our soul exists to serve as a facility for our true self, allowing us to learn from our past mistakes, so we can realize the importance of choosing The Love as our main priority. Spiritual growth then occurs as we let The Love open our hearts on Earth and our true self, our spirit, becomes brighter, as The Love dissolves our limiting patterns and negativities. Our true self is naturally brought closer and closer Home to where we belong.

87. If we think we are going to be able to surrender our ego by our doing, through our efforts, or by our reaching for a state of spiritual perfection, then perhaps we are just fooling ourselves. No

matter how perfect we become, we will still have to eventually surrender that level of perfection because the spiritual journey is not about how perfect we can become. It is not about how humble we can be or what great acts of kindness and service we can perform. Neither is it about how well we can fast, pray or meditate through the night. In fact, in truth, it is not even about 'us.' It is all about True Source's complete Love. The irony is that however good we get, even if 'we' become the best of the best, we will still have to surrender because the 'I' is still in the middle of our accomplishment. The ego or 'I' may tell us, 'I' will help you to surrender, but, it is a joke to think that the ego is interested in surrendering itself. When it comes down to it, to survive and stay in control, the ego will run for the hills and find hiding spots we did not even know exist.

88. When we are willing to let The Love open our hearts, we begin the journey of feeling, trusting, enjoying and accepting True Source's Love in a deeper and more continuous way. Then, The Love and Light of True Source takes care of everything. Yes, everything! True Source's Love is always available, giving us the best of the best, waiting to bring us Home to where we belong: Home, where we are no longer separated from our Source. This is only possible when we allow True Source to take care of everything. On our own, we would not possibly be able to take care of everything, since we do not even have a clue as to what 'everything' is!

89. Spiritual surrender is not meant to be a great challenge or something you have to achieve by your effort. It is simply a joy based on your relationship with The Love and Light of True Source. Only The Love is and only The Love can be the vehicle that brings us Home, back to being our true self. Why? Because we originated from True Source's Love. True surrender involves letting The Love help us to surrender our whole heart and whole being, which includes our whole journey since we first separated from True Source. We cannot begin to know what that all is, especially from the perspective called 'I.' And that is why it is so important to surrender our false thinking that we know, so we can begin the process of "letting The Love accept us and help us." We have to realize that The Love has always been waiting for us and we have been resisting the process because of attempts to be the one in charge of surrendering.

90. When our whole heart and whole being are expressing our

deepest gratitude to True Source, accepting The Love of True Source, then we are on the path of ultimate joy. Then we live, and have pure gratitude, for the opportunity to let True Source do what True Source wants to with us. We realize that all The Love wants is to Love all of us completely, so that all of our karmic accumulations can be dissolved, and True Source can bring us Home to where we belong... as part of The Love, never again be separated from True Source. When our spiritual heart learns what it means to prioritize and rely on The Love, then the joy of surrendering to The Love just happens effortlessly, in our waking moments and even while we are sleeping.

91. The path of spiritual evolution is the path of our spirit growing from a dim spark to become an integral part of The Love, living in union with True Source's Will so that who we are as a being, is no longer separate from the Source of Love. This is about our return to our original state and our true nature, the eternally joyful state we once existed in long, long ago, before we separated from True Source. This separation was due to a desire arising to be 'somebody.'

92. Being mindful, or the observer of our process, can significantly interfere with our ability to feel, enjoy, accept and rely on True Source's Love. We train ourselves to be good observers, such that this aspect of our consciousness then witnesses our heart in the same way it observes thoughts or emotions. However, observing our heart ultimately keeps us disconnected from our heart and may block our feeling the direct connection to True Source's Love. Just as being an observer through mindful practice allows us to witness our drama, it may also result in our heart becoming a separate object, which is then experienced from a distance. It is important for us to realize that the part of us that is observing our heart may not fully trust our heart and therefore may not completely trust The Love of True Source. If that observer completely trusted our heart and The Love of True Source, it would submerge into The Love so fast, it would never again be separated from True Source's Love.

93. When we rely on our own ways to evolve spiritually, despite our best efforts and good intentions, we cannot arrive where we 'are destined' to be. When we learn to feel and enjoy The Love, we naturally begin to let go and to trust The Love. And when we begin to accept and rely on True Source's Love, our spiritual evolution can happen at tremendous speed. If we hit a plateau,

it is not because The Love is limiting our spiritual growth; it is because in some way, we are still observing, or controlling, and limiting how much we allow The Love of True Source to give us the best of the best. True Source is incapable of withholding Love, because Loving us completely is the nature of True Source's Love. If ever we feel that we have stagnated, we do not have to look very far to find the culprit; we can just look in the mirror. True Source's Love is always with us, guiding and helping us, supporting the completion of our spiritual evolution.

94. With anything that we do as the 'doer', whether being a witness of our thought processes, or as the one doing a spiritual practice, we are still relying on 'us' as the key to bridge the gap between our state of separation and The Love of True Source. From my experience, this willingness to rely on ourselves is the biggest trap of all, and sometimes can be very subtle and hard to recognize. Even when we think we are not being the 'doer', if 'we' are practicing a technique, then we still believe we are in charge of our awakening, and responsible for our transformation. If we keep thinking and acting as though we are the one responsible, feeling that it is up to us to 'do' something to get from where we are to the place of spiritual completion, then we are being the 'doer', and the result will be illusory.

95. Even if our belief system tells us we are free, we are only free to the extent that our spiritual heart is open and free, free to allow the gentleness of True Source's Love to radiate in all directions without limit. Only when our whole heart and whole being has dissolved in the gentleness of The Love, can we be instruments according to the Will of True Source. That is the deepest meaning of "Let Thy Will be Done." This is the opposite of "I have the expectation and the right that my will be done."

96. A soul that ascends to a higher dimension is still carrying the remaining storehouse of karma or unresolved blockages from its previous journey through time. But in reality, our soul, instead of aligning with the ego and placing its own development above all else, has the blessed opportunity to serve as a facility for our spirit, our true self. In this way, the soul can be helpful in completing the spiritual evolutionary process. Then we are utilizing our soul for the purpose for which it was given, by True Source. But our soul has to first realize the role it is meant to play in the bigger plan. Without this deep inner realization, our soul will continue to align with the ego and act as an independent agent,

thinking its purpose is to climb to achieve a higher realm while carrying the baggage of unresolved karma and blockages on its back. The ultimate lesson is for our whole heart and whole being to continuously choose, accept and rely on The Love of True Source, feeling grateful in every moment and in every circumstance. This allows us to share The Love and Light of True Source to the heart of every being, while all karmic blockages within us and everything that is not of The Love, is being dissolved. Our spirit, our true self, awakens in True Source's Love and is able to fulfill the purpose of our existence. The very core of our heart realizes this truth. The deep inner longing of our spark, our true essence, wants only to become a part of The Love and to return to our original Home.

97. After we have grown in our ability to feel, enjoy, trust and accept True Source's Love, then, we notice the moment when we get pulled out of our hearts into ego games or old conditioning, and it is easier for us to let Love bring us back into The Love. We don't resist, try, observe or interfere with the process. Instantly, we are available to be brought back into the gentle enjoyment of The Love, and this begins to be our permanent Home, rather than a temporary residence. We are awakening, and the gentleness and tenderness of The Love become our standard of what it feels like to be "spiritually normal". The more of us who begin experiencing our heart as normal consciousness, the easier it will become for others to easily flow into a natural state of 'spiritual normality'.

98. It is important for the core of our heart to realize that True Source never wants us separate from The Love. We chose to be separate. True Source's Love has always been waiting, even during our darkest moments, to bring us ba ck to where we belong. In order to awaken and remain in the spiritual flow, we have to allow our free will to choose True Source's Love. We have to realize that this is not a burden or a sacrifice. It is pure joy. Our heart has to realize that when our free will chooses pettiness or when we justify our right to our emotional reactions or mental preoccupations, then we are turning our backs on True Source, turning away from the complete Love that True Source has for us, and for every being.\

99. As we learn to rely on The Love, we also feel safer, and it is easier to let go of our edges, the boundaries that have kept us isolated from being a part of The Love. As our whole heart and

whole being begins to trust The Love on deeper and deeper levels, we realize it is joyful beyond joyful, that loving and trusting True Source is what our true self has been waiting for since time began! Our spiritual journey is designed to fulfil the purpose of why we exist. The spark of Love and Light in the core of our hearts, our true essence, is so grateful to remember this again, so grateful to once again feel and hear the eternal call for our spirit to return Home. We feel only gratitude to have the opportunity to respond to and follow this eternal call, to become an instrument and a part of The Love, to never again be separated from the complete Love True Source has for every being.

100. From the moment we felt our separation, True Source has wanted us to come Home in the here and now, to once again become a part of The Love. This joyful journey of our spirit, our true self, returning to our Source, is what spiritual growth is about, and the reason for our entire journey in form, on Earth. The Love and Light of True Source is waiting to give all of us the best of the best. To benefit from all of the gifts of The Love, we have to be willing to let our hearts feel grateful for what we are receiving. However, our special time on Earth is not just about receiving. It is about the precious opportunity to become instruments of True Source's Love and Light by sharing and letting The Love within our hearts be free to radiate to all beings, so that all beings, without exception, are touched by The Love. Our individual healing is linked to the collective healing of all hearts. The time is now for us to trust True Source, and let True Source's Love and Will have its way, so that we can continue to collectively flow together. Then all of our true selves can awaken. It is time for us to become instruments of True Source's Love and Light radiating the Love and Light to all beings on every dimension in the whole of existence. This is not a duty. It is our joy beyond joys. Our hearts are waking up to the direct connection of Complete Love that our Creator has for every being. And it is time for our hearts to realize that only True Source's Love can set us free so we can fulfil the purpose of why we exist.

Afterword

Our non-physical spiritual heart is the doorway and key to happiness, joy and spiritual fulfilment. Feeling, enjoying, trusting and accepting True Source's Love is how our spiritual heart opens. Our heart opens to the degree that we let The Love dissolve the blockages in our heart. This is the spiritual evolutionary process of how our spirit/true self awakens in True Source's Love.

You may be asking, so where do I go from here? This book was not meant to be a how-to-book. If you are interested in reading a book that will have easy heart enjoyment exercises to follow, I recommend <u>Smiling to Your Heart Meditations</u>, by Irmansyah Effendi. It is important to realize that in order to experience our hearts, there are basic foundational steps that need to be integrated. This book will be a great place to begin.

Open Heart Meditation, by Irmansyah Effendi, is a wonderful way to begin experiencing how True Source's Love dissolves the blockages within our hearts. I recommend downloading a free audio copy and exploring the two sites below.

- www.heartsanctuary.org (A Non-profit organization)
- www.openheartmeditation.org

For those interested in attending Open Heart Workshops, there are six levels that are designed to help us progress through different spiritual stages. We can experience going deeper into the core of our hearts where our inner heart can be experienced. We can also enjoy learning how to become instruments of True Source's Love and Light so our hearts are free to share the gentleness of The Love with all beings. It is a comprehensive curriculum that also includes letting True Source's Love dissolve blockages in the deeper inner layers of our heart, safe opening of the chakra knots, letting The Love cleanse our core channel, self-healing, a safe awakening of kundalini, and developing a well-grounded connection to the Earth. The curriculum provides an opportunity to have a deeper direct connection to The Love and Light of True Source.

Following are some national and international links for workshops. I have also included links for Reiki Tummo Workshops that are spiritually focused on our heart connection with True Source, while teaching how to channel Divine energy for improving the physical, mental and emotional well-being of ourselves and others.

United States

-                                 www.openheartworkshops.com
- Los Angeles   *www.reikitummo-la.com/index.htm*

International

- www.padmacahaya.com

Oceania

- Australia   www.padmacahaya.org.au
- Sydney, Australia   www.reikitummosydney.com

New Zealand

-                                   www.lotuslight.net.nz

Europe

- United Kingdom   www.open-your-heart.org.uk
- Germany   www.herzensbewusstsein.de

Central and South America

-                                   www.santuariodelcorazon.com

Asia

- Hong Kong   *www.padmacahaya-hk.com*
- Singapore   www.rtas.org.sg/

I appreciate your taking the time to read <u>The Way of the Spiritual Heart</u>. I trust that your journey will abound in joy as you let True Source's Love dissolve everything that is not of The Love. We can become instruments of The Love and Light, according to True Source's Love and Will. Our deepest purpose on Earth will be experienced as we let The Love fulfil our spiritual evolutionary process. Then, with gratitude and great joy, we can all let The Love of True Source have its Way.

With Love,

Ed Rubenstein

About the Author

Ed Rubenstein received his Doctorate in Counseling Psychology from Florida State University, and holds a Masters in Spiritual Studies from Goddard College, a Masters in Psychology from Radford University and a Masters in Rehabilitation from Florida State University.

He lived and studied in Nepal and India for nearly 3 years. Ed has been in the human potential field for over 30 years and has served as a psychologist teaching body, mind, spirit modalities in university, hospital, non-profit, corporate, and community settings.

He continues to conduct Open Heart Workshops and Spiritual Retreats for the Padmacahaya Foundation, both nationally and internationally. Ed is a founding member of Heartsanctuary.org, a non-profit dedicated to educating the public that our heart is the key to our deepest fulfillment.

Ed enjoys living with his wife in the wonderful Blue Ridge Mountains of North Carolina and they have two grown sons. When he is not seeing clients, conducting workshops or volunteering, you will most likely find him strolling or sitting in the mountains while enjoying nature.

Lightning Source UK Ltd.
Milton Keynes UK
UKOW051951040712

195486UK00001B/42/P